B. P. Pratten

An exact Relation of the Entertainment of his most sacred Majesty William III.

B. P. Pratten

An exact Relation of the Entertainment of his most sacred Majesty William III.

ISBN/EAN: 9783337216726

Printed in Europe, USA, Canada, Australia, Japan

Cover: Foto ©ninafisch / pixelio.de

More available books at **www.hansebooks.com**

AN EXACT RELATION OF THE ENTERTAINMENT

Of His Moſt Sacred Majeſty

WILLIAM III.

KING of *England,* Scotland, France and Ireland;

Hereditary Stadtholder of the *United Netherlands, &c.*

At the *HAGUE.*

Giving a particular Deſcription of His MAJESTY's Entry there, *Jan.* 26. 169¾. And of the ſeveral Triumphant Arches, Pyramids, Pictures, *&c.* with the Inſcriptions and Devices.

Illuſtrated with Copper Plates of the whole Solemnity, exactly drawn from the Original.

By an Engliſh Gentleman.

LONDON:
Printed in the Year M. DC. XCI.

THE
PREFACE.

HAVING often Observed, that Relations of Travels, Voyages, &c. are generally very Acceptable to the Genius of the English Nation, I judged that it might not be altogether Impertinent to give a brief Account of some remarkable Observations made during my Abode in Foreign Countries, especially having Travelled for the space of Sixteen Years through Holland, Germany, Sweden, Denmark, *and other considerable Parts of* Europe.

I easily foresee, that it will be soon Objected, that after so great a Man as Sir William Temple, *who hath already Published a full and incomparable Description of the Policy and Government of the States of the* United Provinces, *it would be a vain Presumption to attempt any farther on that Subject. However, without derogating from his Honour, I have here inserted divers particular Remarks, not mention'd by him, but such as Travellers may make Use of to very good purpose, for whose Information this small Essay is chiefly design'd.*

The Preface.

design'd. And it will be the more eminently Useful at this time, in respect of the great number of English Gentlemen, that now Travel that way. Wherefore I doubt not, but this will be a sufficient Plea to cover me from the Imputation of Vanity, and to make it appear, that what I have here perform'd, is only intended for the publick Service in general, and the particular Assistance of those Gentlemen, who shall hereafter Travel through these Countries. The Lists of the Passage Boats and Wagons in Holland, *with the Hours of their going off, which I have inserted, the Traveller will find extreamly Useful.*

As for the Relation of the Kings Voyage to Holland, *annexed at the end. I Confess indeed, That it deserves to be Written by an abler Hand; but being at that time at the* Hague, *I was induced by Curiosity, to take an exact Account of this so extraordinary a Solemnity, which I did at first for my own private Use, but have now Published it through the importunity of some Friends. The Prospects of the Triumphal Arches, Pyramids,* &c. *are exactly Copied from the Original Draughts taken at the* Hague, *and are the true Representations of them.*

A

A DESCRIPTION OF HOLLAND.

With some Necessary

DIRECTIONS FOR

Such as intend to Travel through the Province of *HOLLAND, GERMANY, &c.*

AS they that confine themselves to their own Country, have not the opportunity to see and observe Rarities in other Parts of the World; so, such as go into Foreign Places, rather Wander at Random, than Travel, who have not the Curiosity to commit to Memory or Writing such Things they meet with, both for their own and others Satisfaction,

&tion, as may demonstrate the Fruits of their Travels.

I confess, all Travellers are not of alike Temper; some delight themselves in Contemplation of the Curiosities of Arts; some are taken with the Varieties of the Works of Nature; others speculate, with a kind of Reverence, the Decays and Ruins of Antiquity; others studiously inform themselves with the Transactions of Modern Times; others with the Government and Polity; others speculate the strange Customs and Fashions of the Places they pass through; to be short, every one labours to entertain the Reader with those Objects and Rarities of Foreign Parts his Genius and Inclination is most affected with.

As to my self, although during the space of 16 Years Travel, I might have enlarged, according to the Curiosity and Opportunity I have had in the rehearsal of many rare and exquisite Things very observable; yet my chief Aim was, to make such Remarks as might most contribute to the common Good of Human Society and Civil Life, in taking notice of the Government and Polity of the several States and Dominions where I have been, *viz*. The *United Provinces*, *Germany*, *Denmark*, *Sweden*, and other Countries, whose natural Temper and Disposition seemed to me most to sympathize with our English Nation, and thereby have an occasion to do some good to my own Country. Expect not,

not, Reader, a like punctualness, as to all the forementioned places, because very many things, which I might have observed, are much agreeing, and so may be referred to what shall be spoken of the Polity and Government of *Holland*; which, for Reasons I shall by and by hint at, is the chief End I aimed at in this Treatise.

We will begin then in the first place with the Commonwealth of *Holland*, and Dominions of the States General, which thô for some years were in a declining condition, and their Forces exceedingly weakened, by reason of that fatal War it managed against *England*, *France*, and the Bishop of *Munster*; unto which, if we add the intestine Divisions of those two Factions the Prince of *Orange* and *Lovestein*, that Politick Body, was so totter'd and torn, as did threaten its utter and total Ruine.

But as Bodies, whether Natural or Politick, after that a violent Fit hath fore shaken, dissipated, and exhausted their Spirits, may recover vigor, and look lively again, if so be the Radical Constitution and Natural Temper be not wholly changed and depraved; even so this Commonwealth of *Holland* hath visibly recovered Strength again, and attained its former Force and Lustre.

We will therefore make some Remarks, as to the Defects and Failings (observed not only by me, but also by others) which that

famous

famous Commonwealth hath of late years been guilty of; which I shall do not out of any Malice, or design of Reflection, the intention of writing this Treatise being simply to insert those Defaults which the wisest of Authors have always judged necessary, not only for the Reformation of this, but of all States whatsoever.

This Commonwealth of *Holland* hath worthily been the Wonder of all *Europe* during this last Age, and perhaps not to be parallell'd in the Records of former Times; for if we consider how many years it was assaulted by the then most Potent Prince of *Europe*, who aspired to no less than the Universal Empire; and that how formidable soever he were, yet they not only maintained their Pretensions, but with uninterrupted Prosperity and Successfulness advanced their Trade, and spread their Conquests in all the four Parts of the World.

Rome it self, though most famous and victorious, yet could not, as is believed, in so short a time do what by this Commonwealth hath been effected. In *India* and *Africa* they soon forced the *Spaniard* and *Portugueses* to yield to them most of their Trade and Possessions: And tho *England* put in for a share, yet they were a long while vigorously opposed by the *Dutch*, and to this hour have enough to do to keep what they have gotten; so that in less than 100 years this Commonwealth

monwealth by their Industry, and Art in Trading, are become so excessive Rich and Potent, that they began to Insult, and would needs be Arbitrators to their Neighbouring Princes and States, and encroach upon their Territories and Dominions.

This drew upon them that fatal War before-mentioned, by which they were sorely weaken'd and brought so low, that except GOD by a more than ordinary Providence had protected and appeared for them, they had certainly been ruinated, and never able to recover themselves again; however, their Pride hereby was much abated: And as Luxury and Lasciviousness are the sad Effects of Prosperity, as well as Pride; so such Vices in a Body Politick and Commonwealth as do corrupt the Radical Humours, by abating the Vigour of the Vital Parts, do insensibly tend to the Consumption and Decay of the whole.

That this Commonwealth hath much recovered its Strength, may clearly appear, if we consider what great Things they have effected since the little time they have enjoyed Peace: They have in less than 7 Years built about 40 gallant Ships of War; They have laid out vast Sums of Treasure in refortifying *Narden*, *Maestricht*, *Breda*, the *Grave*, and many other Places; They have paid vast Sums of Money to their Allies for their Auxiliary Troops, as also 200000*l*. Sterling to the King of *England* to Enjoy their Peace with him. And
be-

besides all this, their Encrease in Riches and Power may be guessed at, by the many stately Houses built within these 5 Years in *Amsterdam*, *Rotterdam*, and other Places; to all which we may add, to what excessive height the Actions of the *East* and *West-India* Company are risen, and the Obligations from the States are so esteemed as to Security, that they can get as much Mony as they please at 2 *per Cent*. Not to speak of the exceeding Encrease of their Subjects, occasioned by the *French* King's Tyranny against the distressed Protestants in *France*, *Alsace*, and other parts of his Conquests; neither will we speak of other Signs of the Encrease of this Commonwealth, as not judging it convenient to commit them to Paper, but will now proceed to shew the Method of Living and Travelling in the Dominions and Places of the States, which, if you do well consider, you may see how happy and easy the Government of *England* is, above that of other Nations.

The *Briell* in *Holland* is the usual place where the Pacquet and King's Pleasure-boats bring on such as come to see the United Provinces; but of late *Helvoet-Sluys* is the place the Pacquet comes to, as being the more convenient Port: Here be sure to furnish your self well with Money. From hence you take a Boat to *Maesland-Sluys* or *Rotterdam*, which, if you go in Company with others, will only cost you 5 Stivers; but if you take one for your

Kings Entertainment Pag:6.

HOLLAND.

your self, will cost 25 Stivers for *Maeseland-Sluce*, and a Ducatoon to *Rotterdam*: The fifth part of which goes to the States for a Tax, they call *Passagie Gelt*; and the other four parts are for the Boat-Men or Schippers, who also out of their Gains must pay a Tax to the States, so that by Computation you pay a fifth Penny to the States for your Travelling either in Boats by Water, or in Wagons by Land.

As you pass by *Maseland-Sluce* you will see a very fair Fishing Village, to which belong near Two hundred Herring Busses, but if you go by the way of *Rotterdam* you Sail by two old Towns, called *Flardin* and *Schiedam*: Yet let me advise you before you depart from the *Briell*, to take a serious view of it, as being the City which in Queen *Elizabeth*'s time was one of the Cautionary Towns Pawned to *England*. The *Briell* had a Voice among the States, but by reason *Rotterdam* hath got away their Trade, by which having lost its former Lustre, is now become a Fishing Town only.

Rotterdam is the Second City for Trade in *Holland*, and by some is called, *Little London*, as having vast Traffick with *England*, insomuch, that many of the Citizens Speak good English. There are in this City two considerable Churches of English and Scotch; And how great a Trade they drive with the King of *England*'s Subjects is evident, for in the year 1674, at the opening of the Waters, after a great Frost, there departed out of *Rotterdam* 300 Sail of English, Scotch, and Irish Ships at once with an Easterly Wind: And if a Reason should be demanded, how it comes to pass that so many English Ships should frequently come to that Haven, It is easily answered, because they can ordinarily Load and Unload, and make returns to *England* from *Rotterdam* before a Ship can get clear from *Amsterdam* and the *Texel*: And therefore your English Merchants find it Cheaper, and more Commodious for Trade, that after their Goods are arrived at *Rotterdam*, to send their Goods in Boats Landward into *Amsterdam*.

This City is Famous, as being the place where great *Erasmus* was Born, whose Statue of Brass stands erected in the Market-place: And although the Buildings here are not so superb as those of *Amsterdam*, *Leyden*, or *Haerlem*, yet the places worth the seeing are, first, the great Church, where several Admirals lie stately Entombed; here you see their Admiralty, East-India, and Stadt-Houses, together with that called, *Het Gemeen Lands Huis*.

From *Rotterdam* you may for five Stivers have a Boat to bring you to *Delft*, but before you come thither you pass through a fair Village called *Overschie*, where the French and English Youths are trained up in Litterature,

rature, as to the Latin and Dutch Tongue, Book-keeping, &c. From thence in the same Boat you come to *Delft* which is Famous for making of Porceline to that degree, that it much resembles the *China*, **but only it is not Transparent.**

In *Delft* **is the great Magazin of Arms for the whole Province of** *Holland*: Their Churches are very large, in one of which are Tombs of the Princes of *Orange*, Admiral *Tromp*, and General *Morgans* Lady, and in the Cloister over against the Church, you have an Inscription in a Pillar of Brass, shewing after what manner *William* the First, that Famous Prince of *Orange*, **was shot to Death by a Miscreant Jesuit, with his deserved Punishment.**

Delft hath the third Voice in the States of *Holland*, and sends its Deputies unto the College of the States General, and to all other Colleges of the Commonwealth. They have also a Chamber in the *East-India* Company, as shall be more largely spoken to, when we shall come to Treat of the State of the said Company.

From *Delft* you may by Boat be brought to the *Hague* for two Stivers and an half; which is accounted the fairest Village in the World, both for pompous Buildings, and the largeness thereof; here the Princes of *Orange* hold their Residence, as also the States General, and the Council of State; here you have

have the Courts of Justice, Chancery, and other Courts of Law. Here you see that great Hall, in which many Hundreds of Colours are hung up in Trophy, taken from the Emperor, Spaniard, and other Potentates with whom they have waged War. Their Council Chambers are admired by all that see them. Many fair Libraries they have belonging to particular Men. The Princes Palace is a most superb Building, and there are many costly Gardens adjoyning to the *Hague*, together with that to the Princes House in the Wood, in which House are in a large Hall the most rare and costly Pictures of *Europe*; there also are those Magnificent and Unparalell'd Gardens of the Heer *Bentham* of *Amsland* and others. I might here speak of the splendor of His Majesties Court in *Holland*, of his Noble Virtues and Valour, of the most Virtuous and Beautiful Princess his Royal Consort, but I dare not, least I should infinitely fall short of what ought to be, and which others have already done before me: And therefore leaving the *Hague*, I shall only tell you that from thence you may for seven Stivers have a Boat to bring you to *Leyden*. *Leyden* is a fair and great City, and the University is very Famous, there being continually in it 1000 Students from all parts, as *Hungary*, *Poland*, *Germany*, yea from the Ottomans Empire it self, who pretend to be Grecians, besides the English, Scots,

Cings Entertainment Pag: 10.

HOLLAND.

Scots, and Irish, who this year were numbred to be above 80.

The most remarkable Things here to be seen, I shall summarily set down: As the place called the *Bergh*, formerly a Castle belonging to the Prince of *Liege* in *Flanders*: The Stadt-house, the University Schools, especially that of the Anatomy, which excels all the Anatomy Schools in the World, a Book of the Rarities whereof you may have for six Stivers; their Physick Garden, and the Professors Closet are all Ravishing in rare Curiosities. But as to their Colleges, they are but two, and very small, not to be compared with the smallest Halls in *Oxford*, neither have they any Endowments, their maintenance being only from the Charitable Collections of the Ministers of *Holland*; neither are any Students to remain longer there than till they attain the Degree of Batchelors of Art: One of the Curators being demanded by me, Why so Rich a Commonwealth as *Holland* is, did not Build and Endow Colleges after the manner of *Oxford* and *Cambridge*; answered, They had not so many able and publick spirited Men as are in *England*, and to deal plainly with you, said he, had we such Colleges, our Burghermasters and Magistrates would fill them with their own and their Friends Sons, who by leading a lazie and idle Life, would never become capable to serve the Commonwealth, and therefore

therefore he judged it much better to put them to Pension in Burghers-Houses, leaving them to the care of the Professors, who are very diligent in keeping the Students at their Exercises, both at publick Lectures, and in their private Houses also, where they cause them punctually at their appointed Hours to come to their Examinations and Lectures, besides those they have in publick. Their Churches are rare, so are their Walks round the City, and the Fortifications very pleasing to behold. Here you have the River *Rhine* running through the City, and falling into it from *Catwyck op Zee*. *Leyden* is very Famous in History for the long Siege it held out against the Spaniard. From hence for 12 Stivers and an half you are brought to *Haerlem* by Water, being 12 English Miles.

Harlem is Famous, in that *Costor* one of their Burghers, first Invented the Art of *Printing*. This *Costor* being suspected to be a Conjurer, was fain to flee from *Haerlem* to *Cologne* in *Germany*, and there perfected his Invention, having in *Haerlem* only found out the way of Printing on one side of the Paper. The first Book he ever Printed is kept in the Stadt-house, for those that are curious to see it. Here is one of the fairest and largest Churches of the Seventeen Provinces, in the Walls whereof there remain to this day sticking, Cannon Bullets, shot by the Spaniards during the Siege thereof. In this Church

are

are three Organs, as also the model of the three Ships that Sailed from *Haerlem* to *Damiater*, seizing the Castle in which the Earl of *Holland* was kept a Prisoner, and brought him away to *Holland*: In the Tower of this Church hang two Silver Bells, which they also brought from thence, and now Ring them every Night at nine a Clock.

Haerlem is Renowned for making the finest Linnen Cloth, Tyffinies, Damasks, and Silk Stuffs; also Ribands and Tapes: They have Mills by which they can Weave 40 or 50 pieces at a time; they make the finest white Thread and Tapes for Lace in the whole World; their Bleacheries surpass all other whatsoever, their Waters whitening Cloth better than any in the Seventeen Provinces: They have a most pleasant Grove like a little Wood, divided into Walks, where on Sundays and Holy-days the Citizens of *Amsterdam* and other places come to take their pleasure. *Haerlem* is the Second City of *Holland*, and sends in Deputies unto all the Colleges of the Government. From hence you have a passage by Boat to *Amsterdam* for six Stivers, but when you are come half-way, you must step out of one Boat to go into another, where you see a stately Palace, where the Lords, called *Dykgraves* sit; every one of these Lords hath his Apartment when he comes for the Concerns of the Sea-dykes and Banks: Here are also two large Sluices, having

having Gates to let in or out Water from the *Haerlemmer Meer*. Near this place about *Anno* 1672, a part of the Sea-Bank was broken by a strong North-West Wind, drowning all the Land betwixt *Amsterdam* and *Haerlem*, which cost an incredible vast Sum to have it repaired. They sunk in this Breach 400 small Vessels fil'd with Earth and Stones, for a Foundation to rebuild the Wall upon, and by unspeakable Industry and Charges at last repaired the Bank.

I come now to speak of *Amsterdam*, which having been the place of my abode for several years, I shall give a more large and punctual account thereof then I do of other Places: It is esteemed by Intelligent Men, the Second City in the World for Trade, and not inferiour to any in Wealth. Certainly *Amsterdam* is one of the Beautifullest Cities in the World, their Buildings are large, their Streets for the most part pleasantly Planted with Trees, and Paved so neatly, as is to be found no where else in any Country, save in some of the Seventeen Provinces. And although, as I have already said, *Amsterdam* may justly be taken for the Second or Third City after *London* and *Paris*; yet it hath neither Court nor University as they have. And now in treating of all the Excellences and Virtues of *Amsterdam*, I shall not hyperbolize or flatter; for before I have done, you shall see, I shall also faithfully

fully declaim against the Evils, Mistakes, and Vices in it.

Amsterdam stands upon 1000 Morgans of Land, encompassed with a very strong Wall and Bastions most pleasant to behold, with a very large Gracht or Ditch for the defence of three parts of the City, the fourth being secured by an Arm of the Sea called the River *Y*, or (as the *English* Men corruptly call it) the *Ty*. There are 13 Churches in this City for those of the Reformed Religion (called *Dutch Presbyterians*) to meet and worship in, with two *French*, one *High-Dutch*, and one *English*, all Presbyterian Churches, who only are allowed Bells, and whose Ministers are maintained by the Magistrate. All these Churches or Congregations make up only a third part of the Inhabitants of the City. The *Papists*, who have 85 Houses or Chapels to meet in for their Worship, make another third part, and have a long Square of Houses for their Nuns to live in, who are not shut up in Cloisters, as in Papist Countries they are wont to do, but may go in and out at their pleasure, yea and Marry also, if they grow weary of a Nunnish Life. These Churches of the Papists have no Bells allow'd them, being look'd upon as Conventicles, and are many times shut up, and again opened at the *Scout*'s pleasure. The other third part of the City is made up by *Jews, Lutherans, Armenians, Brownists* or *English Independants*,

Anabaptists, and the *Quakers*: None of which, as was also said of the Papists, have Bells allowed them, but are accounted Conventicles; and all that Marry amongst them must first be married by the Magistrate, and then (if they please) among themselves in their own Assemblies; neither are any of them admitted unto any Office in the Government, but such only as are of the Reformed or Presbiterian Profession.

The Jews, who are very considerable in the Trade of this City, have two Synagogues, one whereof is the largest in Christendom, and as some say, in the World; sure I am, it far exceeds those in *Rome, Venice*, and all other places where I have been. Within the Court-yard where their Synagogue stands, they have several Rooms or Schools, where their Children are taught Hebrew, and very carefully (to the shame of Christians negligence) brought up and instructed in the Jewish Principles.

Amsterdam, for the wise Statesmen it hath produced, is said to be a second *Athens*; others make it the Storehouse or Magazine of *Europe*, for that it hath such great store of Corn, wherewith it furnishes many other Nations. And secondly, for the exceeding great Magazine of Spices, which in ancient times the *Venetians* brought by Land, furnishing all Parts of *Europe*, but now is done by the *East-India* Company, which not only supplies

Europe

16

Anaba
as was
lowed
cles;
first b
(if th
own
admit
ment
or Pi
Th
the
gogu
stenc
sure
nice,
With
gogu
Scho
Heb
Chr
stru

pro
othe
of
Co
rio
M
the
Pa
Ina

HOLLAND.

Europe therewith, but many places in the *Indies* also. Thirdly, It hath inconceivable Store of all manner of Provisions for War, insomuch, that *England* and divers other Nations send to *Amsterdam* to buy Arms, Buff-Coats, Belts, Match, &c. Yea, here are several Shop-keepers who can deliver Arms for four or five Thousand Men, and at a cheaper rate than can be got any where else; and this they can do by reason of their great Industry in the Ingrossing most of the Iron Works on the *Rhine*, and other Rivers, which run into *Holland*. Fourthly, *Amsterdam* hath more store of sawed and prepared Timber for Shipping than can be found in any one Nation in the World; and this is the Reason why her Neighbor Town *Sardam* is made capable of Building Ships 20 *per Cent*. cheaper than they can do in *England* or *France*: So that both *France*, and *Spain* do many times buy them in *Holland*: As lately the King of *Spain* bought Ten Capital Ships of the two Brothers the *Melts* Merchants in this City. Fifthly, *Amsterdam* is the Staple where the Emperor sells his Quicksilver, not only to the Spaniard, to use in his Mines in the *Indies*, but for the making of *Cinoprium* or *Vermillion*, with which *Amsterdam* furnisheth not only *Europe*, but many places in the *Indies*.

Sixthly, *Amsterdam* is the Market where the French King bought his Marble for *Versailles*,

C

seilles, *Louvre*, and other of his Palaces in *France*: There are such vast Magazines in *Amsterdam*, that a Man would think, that sees them, there were Quarries of Marble near the City Gates. Seventhly, *Amsterdam* hath the most considerable Bank that now is in the whole World; I have compared the Bank of *Venice* with that of *Genoua*, and both their Banks write not of so much Money in two days, as *Amsterdam* doth in one: Further I have compared the Bank of *Venice* with *Hamburg*, and find both those Banks fall very much short with the Bank of *Amsterdam*. There are many other particulars I could name, as Arguments to prove the great Riches and Trade of *Amsterdam*, as those vast quantities of Wines, and Brandy-wines they sell in the North and East Seas, and those vast Countries adjoyning thereunto, from whence they bring Hemp, Pitch, and Tar, and furnish *France*, *Italy*, and *Spain* with the same; and they likewise have much Ingrossed the Copper and Iron of *Sweedland*. I will say no more of her Stores and Magazines, but shall in the next place say something of her Churches, and Charity to the Poor. I will not speak much of her Churches, but only that they are in general large and well Built: In one of them the States have spared no Cost to exceed the whole World in three Things, (*viz.*) an Organ with sets of Pipes that counterfit a

Chorus

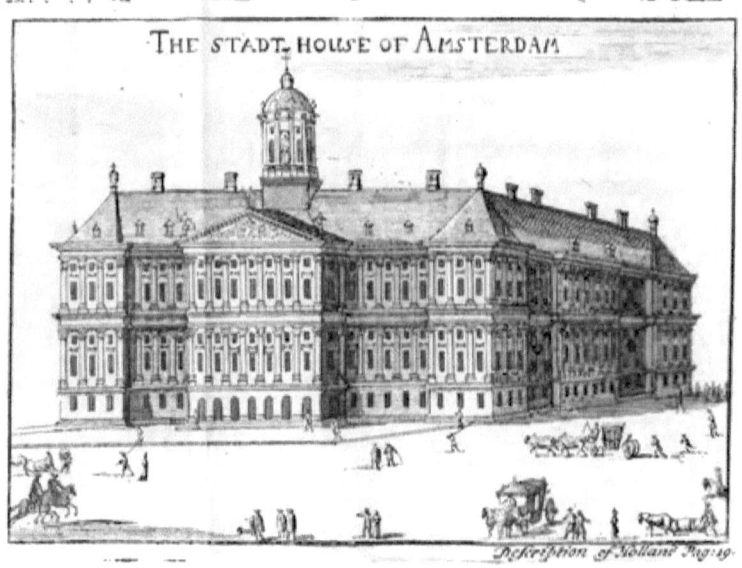

HOLLAND. 19

Chorus of Voices, it hath 52 whole Stops besides half Stops, and hath two rows of Keys for the Feet, and three rows of Keys for the Hands; I have had People of Quality to hear it Play, who could not believe but that there were Men or Women above, Singing in the Organ, until they were convinced by going up into the Organ Room: The Second, Is such a large Carved Pulpet and Canopy as cannot be found elsewhere in the World: The Third, Is a Screen of Brass.

The Stadthouse, or Guild-hall of *Amsterdam*, is deservedly admired and talked of by all the World, it is in Truth a most neat and splendid Pile of Building, and the Reader will not be displeased, I believe, if I enlarge a little in its Description. This Noble Town-House then, is Built all of Free-Stone, according to the Modern Architecture of the Corinthian Order, Adorned with Statues in Brass, and Carving in Marble by the best Masters of the Age. A Prospect whereof see in the following Figure. It is 282 Foot wide, 232 Foot deep, and 116 Foot high, besides the Tower. The Foundation is laid upon 13659 Piles of Wood driven into the Ground; the first Stone of it was laid *October* 28. 1648. In the middle over the Cornish, and just before the Tower, is a very handsome piece of Carving in Marble of 82 Foot long, and 18 Foot high, wherein the City of *Amsterdam* is represented by a Woman,

man, on whose Right Hand sits the God *Neptune*, with his Trident, and two Sea-Goddesses bring her the Fruits of the Earth. On her Left, two *Naïdes* present her with Laurels and Palms; and before her two Tritons Dance and Sound their Horns. On the top of this stands an Image of Brass, representing Peace, and one on each side representing Providence and Justice, each Figure being 12 Foot high. And on the back part of the Building to answer, is such another piece of Carving, in Marble also, shewing the Grandeur and Commerce of the City; in the middle sits a Woman, having on her Head the Hat with Wings of *Mercury*; behind her is seen the Masts and Sails of a Ship, and round about her lies all sorts of Mathematical Instruments used in Sailing; at her Feet lie the two Rivers *Y* and *Amstel*, and on each side, the Inhabitants of the Four Parts of the World bring her their Fruits. Here likewise are placed three Images of Brass of the same bigness with the other; that on the top is an *Atlas*, bearing a very large Globe of Copper, on the right Hand, one representing Temperance, and on the left Justice. On each of the four Corners of the Building, over the Cornish, stand four Eagles of Brass supporting an Imperial Crown, all finely Gilt. In the middle is erected a very handsom round Tower, advanced about 50 Foot above the rest of the Building,

the

the Roof supported by Pillars, and adorned with Images; in it hang a very curious Chime of Bells, which at certain times being played on by a Person maintained for that purpose, afford a very agreeable Musick. So much for the out side. And now let us enter, which you may by Seven little Arched Doors, which let you into the Porch, from whence you enter the House by two large Gates, between which opening by Windows, (with Bars of Cast-Brass) to the Street, stands the Justice-Hall for Trial of Criminals, which is Adorned with many curious Carvings in Marble of Ingenious Devices, which would be too long to describe particularly. Below Stairs, within side, is kept the Office of the Bank, where the Merchants write off their Money, the Prisons both for Debtors and Criminals, the Guard Chamber where the Citizens keep the Head-Watch, and where the Keys of the City Gates are kept lockt up in a Chest every Night, and some other Offices. From hence you ascend by a handsome broad pair of Stairs, though not very light, into to the Burghers-Hall, which is 120 Foot long, 57 Foot broad, and 98 Foot high, in the Floor whereof are inlaid in Marble the two Faces of the Terrestrial Globe, and that of the Cœlestial, which ingeniously shews, as in a Map, the Situation of the Countries of the Earth, and the Constellations

tions in the Heavens: Each of which Maps is 22 Foot Diameter. At the end of this Hall is the Scheepens Chamber, where are Tryed all Civil Causes between Man and Man, and in the Galleries (which go round two square Courts on each side the Hall, for convenience of Light) are the several Chambers, or Offices, belonging to the Government; as the Council Chamber, where sit the Common Council of the City, who make Laws, choose the Burghermasters, and Scheepens, Deputies for the States, &c. The Burghermasters Chamber, who sit there daily to Administer the Government: The Burghermasters withdrawing Room: The Scheepens Extraordinary Chamber: The Treasury Chambers, Ordinary and Extraordinary: The Chamber of Accounts: That of the Commissioners for Bankrupts: Another for the Commissioners for Tryal of small Causes, like our Court of Conscience: And one for the Commissioners of the Hospitals; with two or three more belonging to the several Secretaries, all which are beautified with fine Paintings, and ingenious Devices carved in Marble over the Door of each Chamber; to give a particular Description of which would take up a Volume, which is not agreeable to what I here pretend, these being only short Remarks to put young Travallers in mind of what is most worthy their Observation. I shall only therefore say in general, that it

HOLLAND.

is already a very noble, beautiful, and costly Building, and is a sufficient intimation of the Richness of the City, but should they finish it within side as they pretend, by Painting the Ceilings, and Facing the Walls with Marble, &c. it would make it incomparably the finest and costliest in the World. Over these Chambers, in the second Story, is kept a large Magazine of Arms, which takes up one Angle of the Building, and is very compleatly Furnished; the Arms are all kept in Presses shut up, to avoid the injury of the Weather; the rest of the House above is not used, or Furnished at all. One thing I must not omit, and that is, That there are Eight Cisterns of Water kept always full at the top of the House, which by Pipes may be let down into every Room, to quench any accidental Fire; and the Chimneys are all lined with Copper, the former Stadthouse having been Burnt down by Accident.

I shall now proceed, and speak of their Alms-houses, and of the Government of the Poor, of their Prisons, and Houses of Correction. This City is said to have 20000 Poor every day at Bed and Board. The Alms-houses are many, and look more like Princes Palaces than Lodgings for Poor People: First, there are Houses for Poor old Men and Women, then a large square Palace for 300 Widows, then there are Hospitals for Boys and Girls, for Burghers Children,

dren, and for Strangers Children, or those called Foundlings; all these Boys and Girls have every Sunday, and other days of Worship, two Doites given them by the Fathers of these Houses, the which the Children put into the Deacons Bag when they gather for the Poor in the Churches: Then there is an Hospital for Fools, and a Bedlam: There are Houses where common Beggers, and Gamesters, and frequenters of Tap-houses are kept hard at Work: There is also a House called, the Rasp-house, where petty Thieves, and such as slash one another with Knives, such as beg with cheating Devices, Women with fained great Bellies, Men pretending to have been taken by the Turks, others that pretend Wreck at Sea, and such as Beg with a Clapper, or a Bell, as if they could not Speak or Hear, such as these are kept hard at Work, Rasping every day 50 pounds between two of them, or else are beaten with a Bulls Pissel, and if yet they Rebel, and wont Work, they are set in a Tub, where if they do not Pump, the Water will swell over their Heads: Then there is a House where Whores are kept to Work, as also dis-Obedient Children, who live Idle, and take no Course to maintain themselves; likewise Women commonly drinking themselves Drunk, and Scolds; all these sorts of Hospitals, and Alms-houses are stately Buildings, richly Adorned with Pictures, and their
Lodgings

Lodgings very neat and clean. In some, of the Boys and Girls Hospitals there are 1500, in some 800, and in some 500 in a House; then they have Houses where a Man or a Woman may have their Diet, Washing, and Lodging for his Life, giving a small Sum of Money; these are called *Brouders* Houses. The Alms Children of this City are held in such Veneration and Respect, that a Man had as good strike a Burghermasters Child as one of them. These Children are permitted to Travel in any of the Treckscuts, or Passage-Boats, freely without Money: These Hospitals are Governed by Men and Women, as are of an unspotted Life, and reputed to be Rich, Devout, and Pious: It is very observable, that the Women govern their Women Hospitals, better than the Men do theirs; yea, it is a general Observation in this Country, that where the Women have the direction of the Purse and Trade, the Husband seldom prove Bankrupts, it being the property of a true Born Holland-Wife presently after Marriage, to apply her self wholly to her Business; but I forbear to say any more of the Dutch-housewives, for fear of displeasing our English Dames, not so much addicted, at least not so generally bred up to Industry; But to return to the Acts of Charity of *Amsterdam*, the which is so extraordinary, that they surpass all other Cities in the World, for they are daily and hourly giving to the Poor, every

House

House in *Amsterdam* hath a Box hanging in a Chain, on which is Written, *Think on the Poor*, so that when any Merchant sells Goods, they commonly conclude no Bargain, but more or less is put in the Poors Box; these Boxes are lockt up by the Deacons, who once a quarter go round the City, and take the Money out of the Boxes. Then twice a Week there are Men belonging to the Hospitals that go round the City, and ring a Bell at every House, to know what the Master or Mistriss of the House will give to the Box, who generally give not less than two Stivers. Then every first Wednesday of the Month, the Deacons in their turn, go round the City, from House to House, to receive what every House-keeper will give to the Poor, then on the Week before the Sacrament is given, a Minister, with an Elder, goes round the City to every House where any Members of the Presbiterian Religion live, and there ask if any differences be in the Family, offering their Service to reconcile them; also to instruct and prepare such as are to receive the Sacrament: At this time a Minister may be seen to go into a Taphouse or Tavern, for which at another time he would be counted a Wine-Bibber, and the worst of Reprobates: At this time while these Ministers and Elders go about the City on their Visitations, the People take an occasion to give to the Poor. And here I ought

ought not to omit telling you of their great Charity to the distressed French Protestants, who are here in great Numbers. They maintain no less than 60 French Ministers, and unto many Handicraft Tradesmen, and makers of Stuffs, and Cloth, they lend Sums of Money, without Interest, to buy Working Tools, and Materials for their Work; but this is no other then they formerly did to the Poor distressed Protestants of *Ireland* and *Piemont*; and their Charity was not a little that they gave to *Geneva* towards the Building their Fortifications; and here give me leave to tell you, what King *Charles* II. said of the Charity of *Amsterdam*, when the Duke of *Lotherdal*, hearing that the Prince of *Orange*'s Army was not able to oppose the French from advancing so near to *Amsterdam*, the Duke jearingly said, *That Oranges would be very scarce in* Holland, *after* Amsterdam *should fall into the French Hands to plunder.* To which His Majesty said, *That he was of Opinion, that God would preserve* Amsterdam *from being destroyed, if it were only for the great Charity they have for the Poor*, the which put the Duke out of Countenance; I will say no more of their Charity, only this, that they leave no Stone unturned to bring Monies into the Poors Stock; they make the Stage-players pay 80000 Gilders a year to the Poor; there is not a Rope-Dancer, Poppet-Player, or any of that sort of unnecessary Vermin which

frequent

frequent Fairs, but pay the third Penny to the Poor, which is carefully looked after, by placing an Alms-man at the Door of the Booths, to see that they cheat not the Poor of their share. I shall now in the next place say something of the Clergy, I mean those called, *The States Clergy*, for the States are absolutely Head of their Church; and when any Synod of Divines meet, two of the States are always present to hear that they debate nothing relating, or reflecting on the Government, or Governors; if they do, presently the States cry, *Ho là miju Heeren Predicanten*, and if their Ministers meddle with any thing relating to the Government in their Pulpits, they send them a Brief, (which some call a pair of Shooes) to quit the City, and sometimes Imprison them to Boot; but if they behave themselves quietly and well, as they ought to do, they then are respected by the People as Gods upon Earth: They have a Form of Prayer sent them how they shall Pray for the States, and Stadtholder, nor must they meddle with any other Religion in the Country, because all sorts are Tollerated, at least Connived at by the Magistrates. All those called the Presbiterian Ministers, or States Clergy, are obliged under a Forfeiture to have done Preaching and Praying by Eleven of the Clock in the Forenoon on Sundays, because then the Scheepens go to the Stadthouse, to Marry the

the Jews, Papists, and Lutherans, and others that may not marry after the Calvinistical Form; and the reason why the States thus marry them first according to Law, is to render their Children Legitimate, but they may marry again afterwards as they please themselves: None may marry until they have made their appearance at the Stadthouse before the Lords; where, if the Parties be agreed, the Preachers marry the *Calvinists*, and the Scheepens marry all the rest, who differ from the Religion established by Law.

When one dies, the Friends dare not bury the Corps until it hath lain three days open in the Coffin, that the Friends and Relations of the deceased may be satisfied that the Party hath not been murdered, or reported to be dead when alive; after three days, the Corps must be brought to the Church before the Bell ceaseth tolling, which is at two, for if you keep the Body untill half three, then the Church Doors are lock'd, and for the first half hour must be paid 25 Gilders, and for the second 50, and so until six, then they may amerse you as much as they please.

There are many rich people who make that default on purpose, that they may have solemn occasion of giving to the Poor, as I knew once an English Merchant did.

The next thing I shall speak of, is the method which the States observe in ordering their

their Maritime Affairs, one of the greatest Mysteries in their Government: The States General divide their Admiralty into Five Courts, which they call Chambers. The First is *Rotterdam*, (which is the Chamber call'd the *Maese*,) and hath the Admirals Flag.

Then *Amsterdam*, which hath the Vice-Admiral's Flag; and *Zealand* hath the Rear-Admiral's Flag; the other Two Chambers are those in *North-Holland* and *Friesland*. Each of these Five Chambers have their Admirals, Vice-Admirals, and Rear-Admirals, apart from the States-Generals Flags; so that when the States have occasion to set out a Fleet of an Hundred Ships, more or less, every Chamber knows the number they must provide for their proportion, though in regard of its Opulency, *Amsterdam* frequently helps her Neighbours, and adds two, or more, Ships than their share comes to. These Chambers have lately built 36 Men of War, and now are building of 7 more; and all this is done without noise, every one building their proportion: And they have admirable methods in preserving their Ships when built, and their Magazines are in good order, every Ship having an Apartment to lay up all its Equipage in; and at the top of their Magazines are vast Cisterns, which are kept constantly full of Water, having Pipes into every Apartment to let it down upon any accident

HOLLAND. 31

accident of Fire. And there is in their Magazines a Nursery Room, where a Woman keeps an Office, to feed at certain hours of the day a great number of Cats, which afterward hunt among the Stores for Mice and Rats. This great Magazine in *Amsterdam* was built in the time of *Cromwell*, in the space of 9 months and 14 days, in which time the Lords of the Admiralty gave the Workmen *drinkgelt* as they call it, to incourage them to work more than at an ordinary rate. At this time, the biggest Man of War the States had was the *Amelia*, in which the famous Admiral *Trump* was kill'd; she was a Ship of no more than 56 Guns, afterward made a Fire-ship. But the States quickly discovered their want of great Ships, and therefore built, the same year, 20 Men of War, from 50 to 80 Guns: But the great Ships built at *Amsterdam*, had like to have proved of no use, had not the ingenious Pensionary *de Wit* found out a device to carry them over the *Pampus*, betwixt those they call Water Ships.

The Admiralty have an excellent method in setting out their Fleets, they neither press Soldiers nor Seamen, all go voluntary at the beating of a Drum, each Captain providing Men and Provisions for his Ship, who, after they have received Orders from the Lords to the Equipage-Master to equip out their Ships, and receive the Provisions of War, then

then the States send aboard each Ship a Chaplain, and Check-master, who take care of the provision of War, and see that the Seamen have the States Allowance, and wholesom Food: And great care is taken by the Lords, that both Captains and Seamen receive their Pay punctually for the time they are in the States Service: And for the incouraging their Seamen, there is plaistred on a Board, hanging by the Foremast, the several Rewards to such as either take or fire a Flag-ship, or take or sink any other Ship of the Enemies: Also what Pensions a wounded Seaman shall have, if maim'd or disabled in the States Service, &c.

The Lords of the Admiralty follow the same methods which the States-General observe, as to their Land Obligations, and go through this great Charge by the good Management of their Credit; for though it be true, that they are indebted great Sums of Money, yet they never want a Supply, nay, Moneys are often forced upon them by rich Merchants, who send in their Moneys, and only take the Admiralties Obligations, with which they afterward pay their Customs, when their Ships arrive, at which time the Admiralty allows them Interest for the time they have had their Money: And this is it that makes the Admiralties Obligations more valued than ready Money, for it saves the trouble of telling: And such is the Credit

of

of the Admiralty, that when they have occasion for any Goods, the People strive to furnish them, and rather take their Obligations than Money, because they get Interest; and all other Assignments upon the Admiralty are very punctually paid, and without Exchequer Fees; no they are Sworn Officers, who are forbid to receive any Monies for Fees, being contented with the Sallery they have of the States. And their methods used at the Custom-house for loading or unloading Ships are very easie, insomuch, that the Women generally have the charging and discharging the Ships at the Custom-house, which is a great Policy in the States to make Trade easie for the Encouragement of the Merchants: And the Admiralty are very grateful and generous unto their Commanders; if any of their Admirals, or Captains are kill'd at Sea, and have done any considerable Service, they then Eternize their Memories with lasting Trophies of Honour, as you may see by those Stately Monuments of *Trump*, *Updam*, *de Ruiter*, the *Eversons*, and others; nor are they sparing in bestowing large Gifts and Pensions on the Widows, and Children of those as have served them Faithfully and Valiantly in the Wars, whilst the Treacherous and Cowards meet with the severity they deserve; I might here in the next place, inlarge and tell you of the excellent methods they have in Building, and

pre-

preserving their Ships when Built, but I shall refer you to that excellent Peice written by the *Heer Witsen* on that Subject. And shall now in the next place say something of their Famous Company, called the *East-India* Company of the *Netherlands*; this Company is said to be a Commonwealth within a Commonwealth, and it is true, if you consider the Soveraign Power and Privileges they have granted them by the States General, and likewise consider their Riches, and vast number of Subjects, and the many Territories and Colonies they possess in the *East-Indies*, they are said to have 30000 Men in constant Pay, and above 200 Capital Ships, besides Sloops, Ketches, and Yachts. This Company hath by their Politick Contrivances, and Sedulous Industry possessed themselves of many Colonies formerly belonging unto the Spaniards, Portuguises, and divers Indian Princes, and as good Christians have been at great Charge in Planting the Gospel of Christ in many parts there, Printing in the Indian Language Bibles, and Prayer Books, and Catechisms, for the Instruction of the Indians, maintaining Ministers and School-masters, to inform those that are Converted to the Christian Faith: And now, because I have said that this Company is so considerable, and as it were a Commonwealth apart, I will demonstrate it to be so; first by their Power, Riches, and Strength

in

HOLLAND.

in the *Indies*, secondly, what Figure they make in *Europe*, and this very briefly, for if I should speak of every particular, as to their Possessions in the *Indies*, it would swell into many Volumes, but I will only begin with them at the *Cape de bonne Esperance*, where they have built a Royal Fort, in which they maintain a Garison of Soldiers to defend their Ships which come there to take in fresh Water: From thence let us take a view of them in the Island of *Java*, where they have built a fair City called *Battavia*, and Fortified it with Bastions, after the mode of *Amsterdam*. This City is the place of Residence of their grand Minister of State, called the General of the *Indies*, he hath allowed him Six Privy Counsellors in Ordinary, and Two Extraordinary, these govern the Concerns of the Company throughout the *Indies*, and they make Peace and War, send their Ambassadors to all parts thereof, as occasion requireth. This General hath his Guards of Horse and Foot, and all sorts of Officers and Servants, as if he were a Soveraign Prince, the whole Expence whereof is defrayed out of the Companies Stock. This General hath much of the direction of *Bantam*, and other parts of the Island of *Java*: From whence let us take a view of them in their great Possessions in the *Molucca* Islands, and those of *Banda*, where they are become so formidable, that they look as if they aimed at the

Sove-

Soveraignty of the South Seas:
alſo a great Trade in *China*, and
whence let us return to the Iſland
rra, and on the Coaſt of *Bengal*
they have ſeveral Lodges: In *Perſi*
likewiſe great Commerce, and a
derable, that they wage War
mighty Monarch if he wrongs th
Trade. They alſo have ſeveral C
Lodges on the Coaſt of *Malabar*
mandel, and in the Country of
Mogul, and King of *Galcanda*,
pally let us behold them in the ri
Zeylon, where they are Maſters o
Country, ſo that the Emperor, or K
Iſland, is forced to live in the
whilſt this Company poſſeſs the
lomba, and other the moſt conſide
riſons of that Iſland: It is ſaid, tha
pany hath there in their pay 360
and at leaſt 300 Guns Planted in
and Gariſons; in a word, they a
Maſters of the Cinnamon, but o
Spices except Pepper, and that t
alſo have, had it been for their
Ingroſs, but they wiſely foreſaw
Engliſh would be a block in their
fore they contented themſelves to
of the Mace, Cinnamon, Cloves
megs, with which they not only
rope, but many places in the *Indie*
ſay no more of them in the *Indies*.

see what Figure they make in *Europe*. And first to begin with them in *Amsterdam*, where they have two large stately Palaces, one being in the old part of the City, and the other in the new; in that of the old part of the City they keep their Court, and there sits the Resident Committee of the Company, where also they make the Sales of the Companies Goods. There for six years the grand Council, or Assembly of the Seventeen, do meet, and after six years are expired, the grand Council of the Seventeen do assemble at *Middelburg* in *Zealand* for two years, and then again return to *Amsterdam*; the other lesser Chambers of *Delft*, *Rotterdam*, *Horne*, and *Enchuysen* never having the Assembly of the Seventeen in their Chambers, so that only *Amsterdam* and *Zealand* have the Honour of that grand Council. I will therefore crave leave to describe unto you the Chamber of *Amsterdam*, it being the most considerable of the Chambers belonging to this Famous Company: In their House or Palace, within the old City, are many large Offices or Apartments; as first, on the lower Floor is their Parliament Chamber, where the Seventeen do sit; next to this Chamber are several fair Chambers for the Committees to sit in. They have also a Chamber of Audience, where they do receive Princes or Ambassadors, or other great Men as have occasion to speak with them. In one of these

Chambers are the Arms of several Indian Princes they have Conquered. On the same Floor is their Treasury Office, where their Receivers sit and receive Money, and Pay out the Orders or Assignments of the Company; near to that Chamber sits their grand Minister, the Heer *Peter van Dam*, who is said to be a second *John de Wit* for Parts, tho' not so in Principle: This great Minister is a Man of indefatagable Industry, and labours Night and Day in the Companies Service; he Reads over twice the great Journal Books which come from the *Indies*, and out of them makes Minutes to prepare matters of Concern necessary to be considered by the grand Council of Seventeen, and by the inferiour Committees of the Company, and prepares Instructions and Orders to be sent to their Chief Ministers in the *Indies*; I could say many more things of his great Worth and Virtues, but shall forbear left I should be judged a Flatterer: Over-against this great Ministers Office sit in a Chamber many Clarks, or under Secretaries, who receive from this Minister their Orders of Dispatches in the Affairs of the Company; and next to this Chamber is a Register Office, where are kept the Journal Books of the *Indies*, where you may see the Names of all the Men and Women that have ever served the Company in the *Indies*, with the time of their Death, or departing the Companies Service: Then

next

next to that is a Council Chamber, where the Residing Chamber, or Committee of the Company always sits; then ascending up Stairs, there sit their Book-holders, who keep the Accounts of all the Transactions of those that buy or sell Actions of the Company, and over against this Office sits the *Heer Gerbrand Elias*, who is the second Advocate of the Company: On this Floor are several large Rooms, in which are great Stores of Pack'd Goods, and also a Room with all sorts of Drugs, Tea, Wax, Ambergreace, and Musk; and on the same Floor is a Chamber where the Commissioners sit, who govern the Pack-houses; and next to them sit their Clerks, who keep the Registers of the Sales of the Companies Goods: And on the same Gallery or Floor, is a Chamber where are kept the several Books of Divinity, Printed in the Indian Language, that are sent to the several Colonies of the Company: And at the end of this Gallery is a Magazine full of Medicaments and Instruments for Barber Chirurgeons Chests, to furnish the Companies Ships and Garisons in the *Indies:* Then ascending up another pair of Stairs, there are several large Magazines of Nutmegs, Cloves, Mace, and Cinnamon; and in a long Gallery are many Men at Work sorting of Spices fit for Sale: Then ascending up another pair of Stairs there are many Rooms full of Spices; then descending into the Court-yard, there is Guard Chamber, where every Night the House-keeper hath a Watch, and on the other side of the Gate, there is a Chymist, who with his Men prepares Medicaments for the *Indies*; adjoyning to this Court-yard is their Ware-house and Pack-house for Pepper and Grofs Goods; but before I leave this House in the old part of the City, I must say something of the manner or method used in the Transactions of the Jews and others, who make a Trade of Buying and Selling the Actions of the Company, the which is a great Mystery of Iniquity, and where it inricheth one Man, it ruins an hundred. The Jews are the chief in that Trade, and are said to Negotiate 17 parts of 20 in the Company; These Actions are bought and sold four times a day, at 8 in the Morning in the Jews-street, at a 11 on the Dam, at 12 and at one a Clock upon the Exchange, and at six in the Evening on the Dam, and in the Colleges or Clubs of the Jews until 12 at midnight, where many times the crafty Jews, and others have contrived to coin bad News to make the Actions fall, and good News to raise them, the which Craft of doing at *Amsterdam* is not taken notice of, which is much to be wondred at, in such a Wise Government as *Amsterdam* is; for it is a certain Truth, they many times spread Scandalous Reports touching the Affairs of State, which pass amongst the Ignorant for Truth.

HOLLAND.

I shall now in the next place say something of their Palace, or Magazine, in the new part of the City, the which may more properly be called an Arsenal: It is a Building so superb, that it looks more like a Kings Palace, than a Magazine for Merchants: I have measured the Ground on which this Arsenal stands, which I find to be 2000 Foot, and square every way, reckoning the Motes, or Burgals, about it. I remember the Ingenious Sir *Joseph Williamson* measured the two Rope-Alleys, by telling the Stone-Figures in the Wall, and found them to be 1800 Foot long, the like whereof is not to be seen in the World. On the backside of this Rope-Alley lies a store of Five Hundred large Anchors, besides small ones; in this Arsenal they build the Ships belonging to this Chamber: And here are all sorts of Work-houses for the Artificers that serve the Company. And in a Chamber next to the Joyners Office, is a model of a Ship, they now build their Ships by, which cost 6000 Gilders. When a Man beholds the great Stores of Timber, Cordage, and the Provisions of War in their Magazine, a Man would think there were enough to furnish a whole Nation: In this Arsenal the Ships unload their Goods, laid up in several Apartments in the grand Magazine, and afterward is removed to the House in the old part of the City, as there is occasion for Sale.

Sale. In the upper part of this large Palace fit the Sail-makers at work; but on the lower part of this House is an Aparment where the Committee assemble upon occasion of Business: This Arsenal is not to be seen by Strangers without a Ticket from the Bewinthebbers. Now all what I have spoken of these two Houses, or Magazines, doth only belong unto the Chamber of *Amsterdam*. There are yet other Chambers of the Company, who, according to their Quota, or stock in the Company, have the like Houses and Magazines, as the Chambers of *Zealand*, *Delft*, *Rotterdam*, *Horne*, and *Enkusen*. And now I have named the Six Chambers, of which the Company is composed, I shall say something of their Constitution, which is from an Octroy, or Act of the States-General; by which they have Sovereign Power over their Servants in the *Indies*, yea, their Authority reacheth their Servants in all Territories of the States-Generals Dominions: It is Death for any of the States Subjects to be Interlopers against this Company; nor may any, of what Nation soever, that lives in any of the Companies Territories, as Burghers or Servants, return into *Europe* without leave from the Company, only those called Freemen may depart without asking leave to remove: The Grand Councel of this Company is the Assembly of the Seventeen, which are elected

out

out of the several Chambers before named, that is, Eight from *Amsterdam*, and four from *Zealand*; *Delft, Rotterdam, Horne,* and *Enkusen,* send one a piece, which makes Sixteen, and the five lesser Chambers by turns chose the Seventeenth. In the Chamber of *Amsterdam* there are 20 Bewinthebbers, or Committee for Management of the Stock, in ordinary, who are for Life, and have 1000 Ducatoons a Year, and Spices at *Christmas*, and their Travelling Charges, when they go upon the Companies Service. The next Chamber is *Zealand*, which hath twelve Bewinthebbers, who have about 250 *l.* a Year, and travelling Charges, and Spices at *Christmas*. The next is *Delft*, which hath Seven Bewinthebbers, who have only 120 *l.* a Year, and Travelling Charges and Spices at *Christmas*. The other Chambers of *Rotterdam, Horne* and *Enkusen*, have seven Bewinthebbers a piece, and the like Salary, with Travelling Charges and Spices at *Christmas,* as the Chamber of *Delft* hath. These Bewinthebbers are elected or chosen out of those *Adventurers* called the High *Participanten* of the Company: They generally chuse such as are Rich, and Men of Parts and Wisdom, most of them being of the Magistracy of the Country. No Man is capable of being Elected a Bewinthebber who hath not 1000 *l.* Stock in the Company. In a word, this Grand Council of the Seventeen make Laws for the Governing the Company, both in *India*

India and *Europe*. It is they that appoint the Days of Sale, and what Number of Ships each Chamber must send to the *Indies*; and likewise order the Building of Ships, and all other grand Concerns. This Company is worthily esteemed a Wise, Politique, Deserving Company, sparing no cost to get good Intelligence of Affairs, sending Messengers and Expresses over Land to the *East-Indies*. They have their *Spies* and *Correspondents* in all the considerable Trading Parts of the World: They have been so industrious as to gain the Spice Trade, not only from the Venetians, Spaniards, Portuguises, French, Danes, and other European Nations, but have also Ingrossed all the Spices; so that, as I told you before, they sell Spices to the Indians themselves: But this I must say for them, that they are a Generous Company, and gratefully paying Respects where it is due, as lately they have Complemented his Royal Highness the Prince of *Orange*, His present Majesty of *Great Britain*, with an Annual Sum out of the Profits of their Company, to make him their Friend and Protector. Neither are they backward in bestowing Presents upon Strangers that have obliged them, as I could instance in some of our own Nation. They are also very charitable to the Poor, giving them the Thousandth Gilder of all the Goods they sell. And to all the Reformed Ministers in *Amsterdam*

they

HOLLAND.

For Turff, every Tun five Stivers.

For every 20 Gilders in Wood, six Gilders.

For Flesh the Tax often changeth.

There is also a Tax on the Bread.

Then there is a Tax called the 200th Penny, and a Tax called the 8th: Then there are many Taxes in Trade, as that no Man can weigh or measure out his own Goods if sold in gross, but the States Officers must do it. Then the States have a Tax called the *Verpounding* on all Lands and Houses in their Dominions. Then they have a Tax on Seal'd Paper, and a Tax for Registering Lands or Houses; likewise a Tax on Cows, Horses, Calves, and on all sort of Fruit. There are many other Taxes I could name, as a Stiver for every Man that goes out or into any City after the Hour of shutting the Gates. Also you pay for going over some Bridges, and passing through Gates called *Tolbek*, a Stiver for every Person; but Coaches, Wagons or Horses pay more. These I have already named, you will say, are too many; yet I may not forget to tell you, that Milk first pays as Milk; and again if it be made Butter; yea, the Buttermilk and Whay pays a Tax likewise, for all which a Man would think that a People that stand so much upon maintaining of their Liberty should Mutiny, and refuse payment: But this seldom happens; and if it doth,

doth, the States punish them very severely. I remember that in my time there was a Mutiny at *Sardam* about paying a new Tax, whereupon the States sent a Regiment of their Souldiers, and seized the Heads of the Mutineers, and hanged up five or six of them at the Towns end, and severely whipt eight under the Gallows. And in the rich City of *Amsterdam*, if any refuse to pay their Tax, the Magistrates send their Officer to pull off their Doors; and if they remain long obstinate, they send and fetch away the lower Windows of their House, and they dare not put up others, until they have paid the Taxes. However, this is observable, that if any Man will swear he is not worth what he is taxed at, then he is free: But there are many so proud, that they will not let the World know their Condition. I knew a Merchant named *Ornia*, who paid during the War for his 200th Penny, and other Taxes for his and his Wives Children, (having had two Rich Wives) 14000 Pounds Sterling. I also knew an English Anabaptist Merchant, who told the English Envoy in my presence, That he had paid near 4000 *l*. Sterling to the War, and yet the same Man did Grumble to pay his Majesties Consul a pityful Fee or Consulat-Money on his Ships: The reason whereof I once asked him, who answered me, That the King could not raise a Penny in *England* without his Parliament,

and

and therefore much less could he do it in the States Country. Thus these Phanaticks had rather make Bricks without Straw, than pay the least Tribute to their Natural Prince's Officer. Should we in *England* be obliged to pay the Taxes that are here imposed, there would be Rebellion upon Rebellion: And yet after all that is here paid, no Man may bake his own Bread, or grind his own Corn, or brew his Beer, nor dare any Man keep in his House a Hand-Mill, although it be but to grind Mustard or Coffee. I remember one Mrs. *Guyn* a Coffee-Woman at *Rotterdam*, had like to have been ruined for grinding her own Coffee, had not Sir *Lyonel Jenkins* employed his Secretary Doctor *Wyn* to intreat the States on her behalf; and it was reckoned a grand favour that she was only fined, and not banished the City, and forfeiture made of all her Goods. I remember also a Landlord of mine in *Leyden* bought a live Pig in the Market, and innocently brought it home, and kill'd it, for which he had like to have been ruined, because he did not first send to the Excisemen to excise it, and also let the Visitors see that the Pig was free from Diseases. At another time a Wine-Merchant coming to give me a Visit, told me that he had the rarest Rhenish in the City, and that if I would send my Maid to his Cellar with six Bottles, they should be fill'd: Whereupon I sent the Maid only with two

Bottles, and charged her to hide them under her Apron; but such was her misfortune, that the Scouts Dienaers met her, and seized her and her Bottles, and carried her to Prison, which cost the Wine-Merchant 1500 Gilders; and had it not been for the strongest Sollicitations made by us, he had been ruined: So sacred are Taxes here, and must so exactly be paid. And were they not here so precise, it were impossible for so small a Country to subsist: And therefore you may hear the Inhabitants generally say, that what they suffer is for their *Vaderland*: Hence the meanest among them are content to pay what is laid on them, for they say all what is the *Vaderlands* is ours, the Men of War are theirs, the sumptuous Magazins, Bridges, and every thing what is the *Vaderlands*. And indeed in a sense it is so, for they have this to comfort them, that if it please God to visit them with Poverty, they and their Children have the Publick Purse to maintain them; and this is one main Reason why they so willingly pay their Taxes as they do; for there's not a Soul born in the States Dominions that wants warm Cloaths and Dyet, and good Lodging, if they make their case known to the Magistrates. And for the Vagabonds that rove up and down the Streets, they are either Walloons, or other Strangers as pretend to have been ruined by the late Wars.

I

HOLLAND.

I shall now in the next place let you know how excellently the Laws are here executed against Fraud and Perjury, and the Intention of Murders; which Laws were once much used in *England*, as you shall hear hereafter when I speak of the Duke of *Brandenburgh*'s Court.

I shall here instance a few particulars that happened in my time: There was a Spark that made false Assignments on the Admiralty, who tho' related to many of the Magistrates of *Amsterdam*, had his Head cut off; and another who was a Clerk in the Merchants Bank, who made false Posts in their Books, and had his Head also cut off; and all the Portions he had given with his Daughters, the Husbands were forced to pay back, and all his Houses and Goods were sold at his Door in the open Streets: I knew a French Marquis, who swore his Regiment was compleat, and when the States knew that he had not half his Regiment, he likewise had his Head cut off in the Prison in the *Hague*: I also knew a French Pedagogue, a Runagado Monk, who designed to have Murdered his Master Major *Cavellio*, and his two Pupils, young Children of the Majors, and afterward to set the House a Fire to colour the Murder, he had his Head cut off and set upon a Post, with his Body on a Wheel near the *Hague*. I could Name you two other Cheaters, who were severely whipt under the Gallows; and two under Farmers who designed to run away with the States Money.

The Cheat of breaking with a full Hand is not so frequent in *Holland* as in *England*, (where some use it as a way to slip out of Business, and then to live conveniently afterward upon the Estates of other Men) because in *Holland* they are more severely punished when discovered than in *England*: As on the contrary, those that fall to decay through Losses, and unavoidable Accidents which they could not prevent, find a more speedy and easie way of Compounding and Finishing Matters with their Creditors if they be over-strict, than the Custom or Law of *England* doth afford, for the suing out of Statutes of Bankrupts in *England* doth prove many times so pernicious both to Creditor and Debtor through the tediousness of the Proceedings, and the expensiveness of Executing the Commissions, that what by Commissioners Fees, Treats, and other incident Charges, the Creditors are put to such Expences as to be utterly disappointed of their Debt, and the Poor Debtors for ever ruined and undone; I shall therefore in this place give a short Relation of the method used in *Amsterdam* in the case of Bankrupts, which perhaps may be taken notice of by our King and Parliament, for the preventing Disorders and sad Abuses that daily happen in Executing the Statutes of Bankrupts: The Magi-

Magistrates of *Amsterdam* every year Name Commissioners for Bankrupts, out of those that make up a Judicature, like to our Courts of Aldermen in *London*; These meet certain days in the Week in a distinct Chamber in the Stadthouse, over whose Door is cut in Marble the Emblem of Fortune flying away with Wings, and round Chests turn'd upside down, with Mice and Rats Eating the Money-Bags, Pens, Inkhorns, and Paper-Books. There they receive Petitions from Debtors and Creditors, and as occasion requireth, summon the Parties to appear before them, and to lay open the true State of the matter; this done, they either by Authority seize the Bankrupts Books and Effects, or else without any stir and noise leave all remaining in the Debtors Houses, and send thither two Committees to examine the Books, and make an Inventory of the Estate, with power to compose the matter, without giving much trouble to the Parties. If the Commissioners find that the Debtor is come to decay by unexpected Losses, and unavoidable Accidents, to which he did not at all contribute, it is their usual way to propose to the Creditor such amicable and easie Terms, as the Poor Man may be able to perform, alotting sometimes the half of the Estate left to the Debtor, sometimes a third part, and sometimes perswading the Creditors to advance to the Poor Man a Sum of Money to help him

him up again in Trade, upon Condition that he do oblige himself to pay the Creditors all he oweth them, when God shall be pleased to make him able; but on the contrary, if the Commissioners find that a Trader hath dealt Knavishly, and broken with a design to Defraud and Cheat his Creditors, as if it appear that a Bankrupt hath kept false Books, and counterfeited Bills of Exchange, Bills of Loading, or pretended Commissions from Foreign Parts; in such a case they are very severe, and not only seize all the Books and Effects of the Bankrupt, but also Imprison him, and also punish him Corporally; and if the cheat be of an heinous Nature, Sentence him sometime to Death; whereas, if the Debtor be only Unfortunate, and no ways Knavish, then the Commissaries use all the Power they have to force the Creditors to accept the Poor Mans Terms, the which is better for the Creditors than to use the rigour of the Law, in committing the Poor Man to Prison, seeing in that case the Creditors must maintain him in Prison according to his Quality, where if he lies a certain time, and the Creditors be not able to prove the Prisoner hath an Estate, then the Debtor is admitted to his Oath to Swear he is not worth 40 Gilders, besides his wearing Cloths and working Tools, and then he is set at liberty; but in the mean time let the Prisoner have a care not to make a false Oath, for then he is

punished

punished without Mercy, an instance of which happened in my time.

The States having admitted a certain Jew to come and make such an Oath before them, were at the same time informed by the Goaler, that this Jew had been seen through the chinks of the Door, quilting Ducats of Gold, and some Diamonds in his Cloaths, to the value of 5000 Gilders. The States hereupon admonished the Jew to take heed to what he was about to Swear, because the Law was very strict against such as made false Oaths before them, and at the same time caused the Oath, and the Law to be Read unto him; nevertheless the Jew offered to take the Oath, but the Lords not suffering him to Swear, because then he must die by Law, caused him to be taken out into another Room and searched, where they found about him the Ducats and Diamonds: This being told the Lords, they sent for him in, and then Sentenced him to have 60 Lashes under the Gallows, and to be Banished the Country; yet, because the Jew had many Children, they gave the third part of what was taken about him to his Wife and Children, and a third to the Poor, and the other third to the Creditors, which was enough to pay them their Debt: These Commissioners are paid by the States, and have not a Doit from Debtors or Creditors, for all what they do: These Commissioners are also much

much to be commended for their readiness to do good Offices to those Poor Merchants, who having lived honestly, are brought to decay by Losses and Crosses in their Trade; who when they find any such so Poor that they can neither pay their Creditors, nor maintain the charge of their Families, it is their constant Custom, to take their Children from them, and maintain and bring them up in their Hospitals; yea, often also solliciting the Burghermasters on their behalf, to bestow some small Office upon them for their Relief and Subsistance. And here I must not omit to acquaint you, that as the Compounding of Matters in *Holland* betwixt Debtor and Creditor, so as hath been said, is very easie and equitable, so is also their way or method of suing for Debts very favorable, which is after this manner; In the first place, a Note or Summons is left at the Debtors House, and if he neglect to appear, a second Summons is sent, but then if he neither appear himself, or send his Proctor, the Sheriffs order an Arrest against him; and at last, when he is brought before them, if the matter be difficult, it is referred to two or three good Men of the City, and time given him; but if the Plaintiff make Oath, that he apprehends the Debtor hath a design to run away, then must the Prisoner either give Bail, or return to Prison. It is a Remark that I have made in my Travels, that excepting

France

France and *Flanders*, I never saw in any Prison above forty Prisoners for Debt at one time, and in some great Towns, as in *Haerlem* and others, sometimes not one; and the Reason hereof is plain, for you cannot lay a Man in Prison for an Action or Debt, small or great, but you must maintain the Prisoner, so that many times the Charges exceed the principal Debt, and after all, the Prisoner can free himself; whereas the Custom in *England*, encouraged by those Varlets the Pettyfoggers and Catchpoles, of turning a Man into a Prison for a Crown, or it may be for nothing at all, if he cannot find Bail, he may lie and Starve there, is an abominable abuse; as also that of Suborning false Witnesses, which is extreamly cried out against beyond Sea.

And now because I am Speaking of Pettyfoggers, give me leave to tell you a Story I met with when I lived in *Rome*, going with a Roman to see some Antiquities, he shewed me a Chapel, Dedicated to one St. *Evona*, a Lawyer of *Britain*, who he said came to *Rome* to intreat the Pope to give the Lawyers of *Britain* a Patron, to which the Pope replied, That he knew of no Saint but what was disposed of to other Professions; at which *Evona* was very sad, and earnestly beg'd of the Pope to think of one for them: At last, the Pope proposed to St. *Evona*, that he should go round the Church of St. *John de Latera*
Blind-

Blindfold, and after he had said so many *Ave Maria*'s, that the first Saint he laid hold of should be his Patron, which the good old Lawyer willingly undertook; and at the end of his *Ave Maria*'s, he stopt at St. *Michael*'s Altar, where he laid hold of the Devil under St. *Michael*'s Feet, and cry'd out, This is our Saint, let him be our Patron; so being unblindfolded, and seeing what a Patron he had chosen, he went to his Lodgings so dejected, that in few Months after he Died, and coming to Heavens Gates, knockt hard; whereupon St. *Peter* asked, Who it was that knockt so boldly, he replied, That he was St. *Evona* the Advocate: Away, away, said St. *Peter*, here is but one Advocate in Heaven, here is no room for you Lawyers. O but, said St. *Evona*, I am that honest Lawyer who never took Fees on both sides, or ever pleaded in a bad Cause; nor did I ever set my Neighbours together by the Ears, or lived by the Sins of the People. Well then, said St. *Peter*, come in: This news coming down to *Rome*, a witty Poet writ upon St. *Evona*'s Tomb these words; St. *Evona un Briton, Advocat non Larron, Hallelujah.* This Story put me in mind of *Ben. Johnson*'s going through a Church in *Surrey*, seeing Poor People weeping over a Grave, asked one of the Women, Why they wept? O said she, we have lost our precious Lawyer, Justice *Randal*, he kept us all in Peace, and always was so good as to keep us from going to Law, the best Man that ever lived, Well, said *Ben. Johnson*, I will send you an Epitaph to write upon his Tomb, which was,

God works Wonders now and than,
Here lies a Lawyer an honest Man.

And truly old *Ben.* was in the right, for in my time I have observed some Gentlemen of that Profession, that have not acted like St. *Evona*, or Justice *Randal*, I will say no more of them, but wish them as great Fees, and as much encouragement as the Lawyers have in *Switzerland*.

I now come to Speak something of the three Taxes I mentioned in the former part of my Remarks on Taxes, of which the first ought rather to be called an useful and publick Invention, like to that of the Insurance Office in *London*, then a publick Tax, seeing no Man needs contribute to it unless they please, and find his profit by it; but the other may be called Taxes, because the Subjects are obliged to submit to them, but then they are so easie, that what the publick gets thereby, not only lessons extraordinary Subsidies, which many times occasions clamour, when because of their Rarity, and the urgency of Occasions, they must needs be great.

Yet

Yet it is sufficiently Compensated by the advantage and security in the Estates, which private Persons, who are obliged to pay it, reap thereby daily: I am confident, that if the King and Parliament thought fit to introduce some, or all three of these Taxes into *England*, the publick charge of Government might be defrayed with more ease, and with less repining and clamour, than when it must be done by new and high Impositions; however, our Governors are the proper Judges of that.

The first then is an House called the Merchants Bank, which is governed by divers Commissioners, Clerks, and Bookkeepers, likewise an Essay-Master, who judgeth of the Gold and Silver, that at any time is brought into the Bank uncoined: The security given for preservation thereof, are the States and Magistrates of *Amsterdam*. Now if you have a mind to put Money into the Bank, suppose 1000 *l.* less or more, you must go to the Clerks, and ask a Folio for your Name, and then pay in your Money at three or four *per Cent.* according as the rate of the Bank-Money is high or low, or you may buy it of those called Cashiers or Brokers; then get the Clerks to set down in the Folio what you bring in; having done so, you may draw this Sum, or sell it in what parcels you please; but then if you let your Money lie seven years in the Bank, you receive no Interest

for

for the same. If you ask, Where then is the Advantage for the Merchants? I answer, first, you have your Money ready at all times for answering Bills of Exchange, and making other Payments: You are at no charge for Bags or Portage, at no loss by false tale, or bad Money, in no danger of Thieves, or unfaithful Servants, or Fire; and above all, you have the Accounts of your Cash most punctually and justly kept without any trouble, or running the risk of Goldsmith or Cashierers breaking in your Debt; for such is their care, that twice a Year, or sometimes oftner, they shut up the Bank for 14 Days, and then all that have Concerns therein, must bring in their Accounts to the Clerks, who a few Days after, having viewed the Books, acquaint such as have brought in wrong Accounts with their Mistakes, desiring them to return to their Books, and rectifie their Error, not telling them wherein the mistake lies: So that I have known Merchants, in my time, sent back three or four times with their wrong Accounts: But if they begin to grow impatient, and say that they will stand to their Accounts, then they pay a Mulct to the Clerks upon their convincing them of their Mistakes, either by charging too much upon the Bank, or forgetting or omitting what was their due. I knew two Merchants, who having forgot, the one 750 *l.* and the other 220 *l.* in their Accounts, were honest-

ly

ly rectified by the Clerks, so that they sustained no Loss. Besides this care of the Clerks in keeping and stating the Accounts, the Bank is obliged for 5 *l.* a Year to send to every Merchant that desires it, their Accounts every Morning before Exchange-time, of the Moneys written of by them in in the Bank the Day before upon any Merchants Account, and what Sums are written of by others upon their Accounts: So that the Merchants may compare the Banks Notes with their Books, and so save much of the Charges of Book-keeping.

Now if it be objected, That though this be an Advantage to the Merchants, yet what can the Publick gain thereby, seeing the Charges of paying Officers, Clerks, &c. must needs be very considerable?

I answer, That indeed it is a Mystery to those who understand not the thing; but if it were once known and practised, the Advantage of it would appear: For among other things which might be said, the Magistrates of the City take out of the Merchants Bank a sufficient Stock of Money to supply the Lumbert, a Bank that lends out Money, and is Governed by four Commissioners chosen out of the Magistrates, who sit in Court every Day in the Lumbert, which is a large Pile of Building 300 Foot long, containing several Chambers and Magazines under one Roof; in these several Chambers the Commissioners

missioners have Officers sitting to lend Money upon all sorts of Goods, even from a pair of Shooes to the richest Jewel, &c. This is a great convenience for Poor People; yea, for Merchants also, who some times may want Money to pay a Bill of Exchange, and prevents the Cheating, and extraordinary Extortion used by the Pawn-brokers in *England*, *France*, and other Countries. And besides, the Poor have their Pawns safely and well preserved, neither are they punctually sold when the Year is out, or denied under the pretext of being mislaid, as the Poor are often times served by the wicked Pawn-brokers.

There is also another convenience in this Lumbert, *viz.* an excellent way they have of discovering Thieves, and the stolen Goods; they publish two general open Sales of Goods pawn'd, twice a year, that such as will may redeem their Goods, and paying the Interest may have them, although the time be relapsed. Thus much as to the *Lumbert*. I was once, according to my Duty, to wait upon the D. of *York*, at the Bank of Merchants, where shewing his Highness the way of keeping the Journal-Book of the Bank, which is of a prodigious bigness, his Highness was extreamly pleased with the contrivance of preserving it from Fire; saying, that the course they took might be of great use for the preserving Patents, and the Deeds of Noblemens Estates: This contrivance, which perhaps may be thought useful or imitable, I shall therefore describe it: It is a large Fire-stone shaped like a Chest, and set upright in a Stone-Wall, having a large Brass Door of a vast thickness, with Flaps to fall over and cover the Lock and Hinges; into this Chest the Book is drawn upon Rolls, it being of such a bulk and weight as cannot be handed in by a Man, and there it is so securely preserved, that although the House should be burnt, the Book in all probability would be safe. Should I here give an account of the vast Sums of Money that daily are written of in this Bank, I might probably be thought to speak at random, but this I may boldly affirm, that it far exceeds all the Banks in *Europe*, both for Riches and Business, and their Credit is such, that the Italians, French, Germans, and English have great Sums in the same; neither was ever any Man refused his Money in the worst of times.

A second Tax is what ariseth from the just and laudable Establishment of a Register, a Tax which I think most Men will be willing to submit to, except such as design to cheat and defraud their Neighbours, and live by such like Sins and Confusion, and for the most part die with the Curse of the People: This Register in *Holland* begets such assurance and safety in Dealing, that in purchasing of Houses or Land, a Child, though over-reached in the Value, yet cannot be cheated as to the Title. The

The Third and last Tax is that of Sealed Paper, as it is practised in *Holland*. There are many other things might be spoken, as to the Government of *Amsterdam*, but I must not tire your patience. However, one considerable thing I would not pass by, touching the Militia: There are in *Amsterdam* Sixty Companies of Foot, the least of them having 200 Men, some 300, which in a modest account, amounts at least to 15000 Men, in which number neither Jews nor Anabaptists who carry no Arms are reckoned, only they are obliged to contribute to the maintenance of the 1400 Soldiers, who are kept in constant pay, as a Guard for the City, and towards the Night-Watch or Rattel-Watch, who walk the Streets the whole Night to keep good Orders, and tell us every half hour what a Clock it is. There are also upon every Church Tower, Trumpeters, who Sound every half hour; and if any Fire breaks out in the City, they give a Signal on which side of the City the Fire is, and Ring the Fire-Bell; and they have excellent ways on a sudden in such sad Accidents to quench Fire: But I may not inlarge any longer, but hasten out of *Holland*. Though before I leave it it will not be amiss if I give the Reader a List of the Passage-Boats, which for the convenience of those that Travel that way, I have here Collected, with the times of their going off, which they are punctual in observing.

F   Beginning

Beginning at *Helvoet-Sluys*, where the Pacquet-Boat from *England* lies. From whence to the *Briell* there goes a Wagon every Day at 8 in the Morning; the Passage costs 7 Stivers; and the same from the *Briell* to *Helvoet*.

From the *Briell* to *Rotterdam*, and from *Rotterdam* to the *Briell*; there Sails a Boat every Day as the Tide serves.

From *Rotterdam* to *Delft*, and from *Delft* to *Rotterdam*, there goes a Trecht-Scuyt, or Passage-Boat, every Hour, from 6 in the Morning to 8 in the Evening.

From *Delft* to the *Hague*, and from the *Hague* to *Delft*, the Boat goes every half Hour.

From *Delft*, and from the *Hague* to *Leyden*; In the Morning at 5, 7, 9, and half an Hour after 10. In the Afternoon at half an Hour after 12, at $2\frac{1}{2}$, at $4\frac{1}{2}$, and at $6\frac{1}{2}$ daily, as you are to understand all along.

From *Leyden* to *Delft*, or to the *Hague* at the same Hours; In the Morning at 4, 6, 8, and $10\frac{1}{2}$. Afternoon, $12\frac{1}{2}$, $2\frac{1}{2}$, $4\frac{1}{2}$, and $6\frac{1}{2}$; and a Night-Boat at 11.

From *Leyden* to *Haerlem*; In the Morning at $3\frac{1}{2}$, $6\frac{1}{2}$, 9 and 11. Afternoon, $12\frac{1}{2}$, $1\frac{1}{2}$, 2, 4, and 6. Also a Market-Boat every Day before Noon.

From *Haerlem* to *Leyden*; In the Morning at 6, 8, 10 and 12. Afternoon at 1, 2, 4 and 6; and the Night-Boat at 11.

From *Amsterdam* to *Haerlem*, and from *Haerlem* to *Amsterdam*, there goes a Boat every Hour, from the opening of the Gates, to 8 of the Clock at Night.

From *Amsterdam* to *Leyden*, at 8 at Night; and from *Leyden* to *Amsterdam*, at 9 at Night, every Night; and a Market-Boat at 3 in the Afternoon.

From *Amsterdam* to *Utrecht*, from the 15 of *March* to the 15 of *September*, at 7 in the Morning, at 1 in the Afternoon, and at 8 in the Evening. From the 15 of *September*, to the 11 of *March*, at 8 in the Morning, at 1 in the Afternoon, and at 7 in the Evening. And

From *Utrecht* to *Amsterdam* at the same Hours.

From *Amsterdam* to *Gouda*, or *Tergoes*, as 'tis corruptly called; From the first of *April* to the last of *September*, in the Morning at 7; and in the Evening at 8. In *October*, *November*, and *March*, Morning and Evening at 8.

From *Gouda* to *Amsterdam*; In the Morning at 11, and in the Evening at 8. In *December*, *January* and *February*, no Boat goes in the Morning from either place, and only one at 8 in the Evening.

From *Tergoes* you may go by Wagon to *Rotterdam*, or from *Rotterdam* to *Tergoes*, for about 12 or 14 Stivers, which is a convenient

venient Passage for Strangers, there being the least shifting of Boats.

From *Amsterdam* to *Rotterdam*, and from *Rotterdam* to *Amsterdam*; The Market-Boat for carrying Goods goes off at 12 at Noon every Day.

From *Amsterdam* to the *Hague*, and from the *Hague* to *Amsterdam*, the same at 12 at Noon.

From *Amsterdam* through *Muyden* to *Naerden*; In the Summer, from the first of *April*, to the last of *September*, Morning, at 6, 8 and 10; Afternoon, at 2, 4 and 6. In the Winter, Mornings at 7, 9 and 11; Afternoon, 1, 3 and 5. This is a Fortification very well worth seeing.

From *Naerden* through *Muyden* to *Amsterdam*; In the Summer at 5, 7 and 9, Mornings; and at 2, 4 and 6, Afternoons. In the Winter, Mornings, 7, 8 and 10; Afternoons, 1, 3 and 5.

From *Leyden* to *Gouda*; Every Day a Boat goes at 11 in the Forenoon, and on *Saturdays* at 2 in the Afternoon.

From *Gouda* to *Leyden*; Every Day at 11 in the Forenoon, and on *Thursdays* at 12.

From *Leyden* through *Woerden* to *Utrecht*; In the Morning at 9, Afternoon at $12\frac{1}{2}$, and Evening at 9.

From *Utrecht* through *Woerden* to *Leyden*; Mornings at 8 and 12, Evenings at 8.

From *Rotterdam* to *Dort*, and from *Dort* to *Rotterdam*; Every Day a Boat as the Tide serves; as also to *Antwerp* the same.

It will be unnecessary to particularize any more, these being all that Englishmen have occasion for, for whom these Remarks are made, though it will not be improper if I insert the Order for the Post-Wagons, which some for Expedition make use of.

The Order of the Post-Wagons which go between Amsterdam *and the* Hague.

Every Day except *Sundays*, from the 26 of *February* to the 29 of *September*, there goes a Post-Wagon at 6 in the Morning.

From the first of *October* to the sixth of *November*, at 7 in the Morning.

From the 8 of *November* to the 19 of *January*, at half an Hour past 7 in the Morning.

From the 21 of *January* to the 24 of *February*, at 7 in the Morning.

In the great Vacation of the Courts of *Holland*, which is all the Month of *August*, there goes no Wagon in the Morning.

At 12 at Noon there goes a Wagon every Day, *Sundays* and all, throughout the Year.

The Passage in the Post-Wagon for each Person is 4 G. 3 *St.* besides Passage-Gelt. And if any hire a whole Wagon, they may go at what Hour they please, and pay 24 G. 18 St. and Passage-Gelt, provided there be no more than 6 Persons.

And if you are set down by the way you shall be abated proportionably of the Passage, but then you must give notice of it before Hand, and be content to take your place after those that go quite out.

And now having said so much of the States Government, and of *Amsterdam* in particular, it will not be amiss to take notice of some bad Customs and Practices now in vogue in *Holland*, and leave it to the Reader to judge what they may portend: There are Tollerated in the City of *Amsterdam*, amongst other abuses, at least 50 Musick-houses, where lewd Persons of both Sexes meet and practise their Villanies: There is also a place called the Long-Seller, a Tollerated Exchange, or publick Meeting House for Whores and Rogues to Rendezvous in, and make their filthy Bargains. This Exchange is open from six a Clock in the Evening until nine at Night; every Whore must pay three Stivers at the Door for her Entrance or Admission. I confess the Ministers Preach and exclaim from the Pulpit against this horrible Abuse, but who they be that protect them I know not; yet, I have heard some plead for the Tolleration of these wicked Meetings, upon pretext, that when the *East-India* Fleets come home, the Seamen are so mad for
Women,

Women, that if they had not such Houses to bait in, they would force the very Citizens Wives and Daughters; but it is well known, that as Money does countenance, so Discipline might suppress that abuse. The old severe, and frugal way of living is now almost quite out of date in *Holland*, there is very little to be seen of that sober Modesty in Apparel, Diet, and Habitations as formerly: In stead of convenient Dwellings, the Hollanders now build stately Palaces, have their delightful Gardens, and Houses of Pleasure, keep Coaches, Wagons and Sleas, have very rich Furniture for their Horses, with Trappings adorned with Silver Bells. I have seen the Vanity of a Vintners Son, who had the Bosses of the Bit, and Trapping of his Horse of pure Silver; his Foot-Man and Coach-Man having Silver Fring'd Gloves; yea, so much is the humour of the Women altered, and of their Children also, that no Apparel can now serve them but the best and richest that *France* and other Countries affords; and their Sons are so much addicted to Play, that many Families in *Amsterdam* are ruined by it; not that *England* is less extravagant then the Dutch; who as I said before, got such great Estates by their Frugality, whilst they were not addicted to such Prodigality and Wantonness as the English are, whose excess I cannot excuse; nevertheless, the grave and sober People of *Holland* are very sensible of the great alteration that now is in their Country, and as they say, *Paracelsus* used to Cure his Patients of their Disease with a full Belly; so a good Burghermaster desirous to convince his Amsterdammers of their dissolute kind of Life, invited the 36 Magistrates and their Wives to a Feast; who being come, and the Ladies big with Expectation of some rare and extraordinary Entertainment, sat down at Table, where the first Course was Buttermilk boil'd with Apples, Stock-fish, Butter'd Turnips and Carrots, Lettice, Sallat, and Red Herrings, and only small Bear, without any Wine; at this the Ladies startled, and began to whisper to their Husbands, that they expected no such Entertainment, but upon removing of the Dishes and Plates, they found underneath Printed Verses, importing, That after that manner of living they began to thrive, and had inlarged their City.

The Second Course consisted of Bocke de kooks, Quarters of Lamb, Roasted Rabbits, and a sort of Pudding they call a *Brother*; here they had *Dort* and English Beer, with French Wine, yet all this did not please the Dainty Dames: But upon removing away the Plates another Dish of Poetry appeared, which acquainted them, That after that modest and sober way of living they might keep what they had got, and lay up something for their Children.

Then comes in the Third Course made up of all the Rarities of the Season, as Partridges, Pheasants, and all sorts of Fowl, and English Pasties, with plenty of Rhenish, and other sorts of Wine, to moisten them; this put the Ladies in a Frolick, and jolly Humour, but under their Plates was found the Use and Application in Verses, telling them, That to feed after that manner was Voluptuous and Luxurious, and would impair their Health, and waste their Estates, make them neglect their Trade, and so in time reduce their stately and new built flourishing City to their old Fishing Town again. After this was brought in a Banquet of all sorts of Sweat Meats piled up in Pyramids, and delicate Fruit, with plenty of delicious Wines; and to conclude all, a set of Musick and Maskers, who Danced with the young Ladies; but at parting, like the hand writing to *Belteshazzar* upon the Wall, every one had a Printed Paper of Moralities put into their Hand, shewing them the Causes of the Ruin of the Roman Commonwealth, according to that of the Poet,

Nullum crimen abest, facinusque libidinis ex quo,
Paupertas Romana perit.

with an excellent Advice to them, That if they did not quit the Buffoonries, and Apish
Modes

Modes of the French, and return to the Simplicity, Plainness and Modesty of their Ancestors and Founders, their Commonwealth could not long last; but all the Thanks the good old Burghermaster had for his kind and chargeable Entertainment in thus Feasting his Country-Men, was to be Floutted at, and Pasquild, the Sparks of *Amsterdam* saying in all places, That the old Man being now past the years of Pleasure himself, would have none others to take theirs: And here I shall put a period to what I thought fit to observe of the States of the United Provinces, only I will beg leave to say something to the Hollander by way of Advice, *viz.* That now they are in a prosperous Condition, Rich, and at Ease, they would look back and remember what God in his infinite Goodness and Mercy did for them in the days of their greatest Calamities: For my own part I cannot but admire the great Providence of God in preserving them from being devoured by their many Enemies they had in the last War, besides their Enemies at home, some of which particulars as they then happened give me leave to relate. At the time when the French came to Invade the Territories of the States General, it then looked as if God had mark'd out the way for the French to March, by sending such a wonderful dry Season, that the Rivers of the *Rhine*, *Beta*, *Wall*, and other Rivers were Fordable, so that the

French

French only waded throw, and became so Victorious, that in a little space of time (what by the Treasons of some, and the Ignorance and Cowardise of others intrusted with the Militia and Garisons) the French became Masters of above Forty Cities and Garisons, at which time there was nothing to be heard of in the States Dominions but Confusion and Misery, even in the strong and rich City of *Amsterdam* it self, who at this time beheld the French Army like a mighty Torrent coming within sight of the City, and at the same time wanting Water in their Canals, and Burghwalls to ply their Sluces, and such was the scarcity of Rain, that a Pail of fresh Water was worth Six Pence: Thus Heaven seemed to frown on them, as well as the French Army, by the shutting up as it were the Conduits of Heaven, and yet a worse thing had like to have fallen out, for at the same time the Divisions grew so high amongst the Magistrates in the Stadthouse, that it was putting to the Question, Whether or no they should not go and meet the French King with the Keys of their City, to save it from Fire and Plunder; now nothing, in all probability, could save this rich City from falling into the hands of the French, but an immediate hand from Heaven, and it had undoubtedly come to pass, had not Providence caused the French to make a stand at *Muyden*,

den, two hours from *Amsterdam*, at what time the valiant Roman of *Amsterdam*, Scout *Hasselaer*, like a true Father of his Country, opposed the French Party in the Counsel, calling out to the Burghers from the Stadthouse, to take Courage, and rather chuse to die, like old Battavians, with their Swords in their hands, than tamely and treacherously to yield up their City to the Mercy of the French, as some of the Magistrates were about to do; this so incouraged the Burghers, that with great Courage they mann'd the Walls, and Heaven then assisting them with a sudden and plentiful Rain, that they ply'd their Sluces, and drouned the Lands round the City three or four Foot high, in some places, which caus'd the victorious French Army to make a quick retreat, as far as *Utrecht*, else they had paid dear for seeing of *Amsterdam*; thus was *Amsterdam* delivered by the hand of Heaven.

A Second was, when that bloody Duke of *Luxemburg*, who gloried and thanked GOD that he was born without pity or remorse of Conscience, took the opportunity of an exceeding hard Frost, to march his Army over the Ice as it had been dry ground, burning in his way the three fair Villages of *Bodygrave, Swammerdam*, and *Goudse-sluys*; acting there a more cruel Tragedy, and worse, than ever did Turk, for they generally

rally save the Country People for Ransom, but this cruel Prince caused strong Guards to surround the Villages, and burnt Men, Women, and Children together: Thus he began his march, with a design to burn *Leyden*, *Hague*, *Rotterdam*, *Delft*, and all the rich Country of *Rhineland*: And this he might have done in all probability, for, first, the Governor of *New-sluce*, who commanded the Post that should have stopt the French, treacherously delivered up the Fort without firing a Gun; and the handful of Troops then under General *Koningsmark* were so inconsiderable, that they, joyned to the Soldiers under *Pain* and *Vin*, the Governor of *New-sluce*, were not able to make head as could oppose *Laxemburg*'s Army; and at the same time the Prince of *Orange* was with the States Army at *Charleroy*: Now was *Leyden* ready to meet the French with the Keys of their City, and other Cities too, for they had neither Fortifications nor Soldiers to man their Walls: Thus the whole Country and Cities of *Rhineland* were like to fall under the Cruelties and Tyrany of the French, but GOD a second time sent these People Relief from Heaven, first by giving such undaunted Courage to that Great States-man Pensionary *Fagel*, that he forced *Coningsmark* to rally his Troops together, and to make a stand near *Leyden*, offering himself to die at the head of them if there were occasion,

but

but GOD reserved him for a further Good to the Commonwealth, by sending such a sudden Thaw as was never seen before, for in less than ten hours, the Ice so sunk, and such Floods of Snow came down from the Highlands, that the French were fain to make a very disorderly retreat, marching up to the middle for haste, because on the Banks there could not march above four Men a-breast, so they were constrained to leave behind them the greatest part of the Plunder they had robb'd from the Innocent Country People, and the nimble Dutch-men, on their Scates, so long as the Ice would bear them, did shoot down the French like Ducks diving under Water, so that it cost *Luxemburg*'s Army dear, though they had the pleasure to burn the poor People, of which the French afterward wickedly made their boast.

The third was as wonderful as the two others; and although I do not believe Miracles, as do the Papists, yet I say nothing I ever observed looked more like a Miracle than this; to wit, when the English and French Fleet lay before *Scheveling* with a design to land, and the French ready on their March to joyn with the English and other French as soon as they should land, at the same time the Bishop of *Munster* lying before *Groeningen*, and the French before *Gorcem*, so that now all things looked with a dreadful face

face for the States, yet at this very time God sent a third relief, by sending such Mists, and wonderful sorts of Tydes, as so separated the two Fleets, that the English were forced to quit *Scheveling* Shore, and were driven on the side of the *Texel* Road; from whence they were constrained by the season of the Year to retire home: And such were the sudden and great Showers of Rain, that the Bishop of *Munster* was forced in disorder to raise his Siege at *Groeningen*, and the French to quit *Gorcom*. I could add many more Observations of the Providences of God to these People, as the preserving the Prince of *Orange*, His present Majesty of *Great Britain*, from the many treacherous Designs contrived against him from his Cradle; but *Moses* must be preserved, to go in and out before his People. Certainly never young Prince endured so many Fatigues as did his Highness in his tender Years, of which I was an Eye-witness; and had his Highness had the Years and Experience, and such a good Disciplined Army (as now he hath) in the Year 1671. when the French entred the Country, his Highness had given them as good a Welcom as he did at *Bergen*. I will say no more of this Subject, only this, That the Peace at *Nimeguen* was also a very wonderful thing, for that not above eight Days before the Peace was signed, most of the Plenipotentiaries did believe the War would

have

have continued another Year; first, because the King of *Denmark* and Duke of *Brandenburg* prospered exceedingly against *Sweedland*, and totally refused the Propositions of *France*; and secondly, because the French King writ such bitter Letters against the States-General: Yet eight Days after drest a Letter unto the States, in which he calls them his *Good Friends, and Old Alleys,* offering them not only *Maestricht*, but every Foot of Ground they could lay claim to in the World; also giving them new Terms and Conditions as to their Privileges in *France*, by way of Trade. Neither can I forget how speedily and as strangely the French King did quit his Conquered Towns after the Valiant Prince of *Orange* took *Naerden*, which was the first step to the French's Ruine in the States Dominions. I come now, according to promise in the beginning of this Book, to give the Reader some Remarks I made in other Countries where I have been, during my Sixteen Years Travels. To give a full account of all that might be observed in so many Countries, is not a Task for one Man, nor a Subject for so small a Book; I shall only therefore briefly take notice of some remarkable Matters which may in some measure satisfie the Curiosity of my Countrymen, who have not been in the said places, and convince, if possible, all of them, that no Country that ever I was in, affords so

great

great Conveniencies for the generality of People to live in, as the Kingdom of *England* doth. Though I have twice made the *grand tour* of *Germany, Hungary, Italy* and *France*, and after my return back to *England*, travelling a third time through *Holland* as far as *Strasbourg*, and so back by *Francfort* to *Denmark* and *Sueden*; yet the Reader is not to expect I should follow a Geographical Method and Order in speaking of the Places I have been in; that is to be lookt for in the Map, and not in Travels; but only that I mention Places as I found them on my Road, according as Business or Curiosity led me to Travel.

THE first considerable Place I then met with, after I was out of the Dominions of the States-General, was *Cleave*, the Capital City of the Province so called; a fair and lovely City standing upon the *Rhine*, and the Rivers *Wall* and *Leck*. This Province much resembles *England* in rich Soil, and pleasantness of its Rivers. The Inhabitants of the Country would have me believe that they were Originally descended of those *Saxons* who made a descent into *England*, and conquered it; and to convince the truth of this, they shew'd me a Cloyster standing on a Hill, called *Eltham*, from which they say our *Eltham* in *Kent* had its Name. I was made to observe also two places standing upon the *Rhine* near *Emmerick*, called *Doadford*, and *Gronewich*, which according to them, gave the Names to *Dedford* and *Greenwich* in *England*: But many such Analogies and Similitudes of Names are to be found in other places of *Germany*, but especially in upper *Saxony* and *Denmark*. The greatest part of this Province of *Cleave*, and part of the Dutchies of *Juliers* and *Berg*, and of the Provinces of *Marke* and *Ravensbourg*, belongs to the Elector of *Brandenbourg*, the rest belonging to the Duke of *Newbourg* now Elector *Palatine*, and the Elector of *Cologne*. The Inhabitants are partly Roman Catholicks, partly Lutherans, and partly Calvinists, who all live promiscuously and peaceably together both in City and Country. The City of *Cleave* is the utmost Limit of the Territories of the Elector of *Brandenbourg* on this side of *Germany*; from whence his Electoral Highness can Travel Two Hundred Dutch Miles out-right in his own Dominions, and never sleep out of his own Country but one Night in the Territories of the Bishop of *Osnabrug*.

From *Cleave* I went to a small Town called *Rhinberg*, but a very strong Fortification belonging to the Elector of *Cologne*; which lies at two Miles distance from the City of *Wesel*, that belongs to the Elector of *Brandenbourg*. Through *Dusseldorpe*, situated on the *Rhine*, and the Residence of the Duke of *Newbourg*, I went next to *Cologne*, a very large City, called by the Romans *Colonia Agrippina*, and the French *Rome d'Allemagne*.

Cologne is an Imperial City, and a Republick, though for some things it does Homage to the Elector of that Name, and receives an Oath from him. It is much decayed within these Hundred Years, having been much Priest-ridden; a Misfortune that hath undone many other great Cities. The Jesuits have had so great Influence upon the Magistrates, that they prevailed with them to banish all Protestants, who removed to *Hambourg* and *Amsterdam*; so that *Cologne* is become so dispeopled, that the Houses daily fall to ruine for want of Inhabitants, and a great deal of Corn and Wine now grows within the Walls, upon Ground where Houses formerly stood. I dare be bold to affirm, that there is twice the Number of Inhabitants in the Parish of St. *Martins in the Fields*, as there is in *Cologne*; and yet it contains as many Parish-Churches, Monasteries and Chappels, as there are days in the Year. The Streets are very large, and so are the Houses also, in many of which one may drive a Coach or Wagon into the first Room from the Streets: But the Streets are so thin of People, that one may pass some of them and not meet Ten Men or Women, unless it be

Church-Men, or Religious Sisters. The most considerable Inhabitants of the City are Protestant Merchants, though but few in Number, and they not allowed a Church neither, but at a place called *Woullin*, a Mile without the City; the rest of the Inhabitants, who are Lay-men, are miserably poor. There are no less than 3000 Students in *Cologne* taught by the Jesuits *gratis*, who have the privilege to beg in Musical Notes in the Day-time, and take to themselves the liberty of borrowing Hats and Cloaks in the Night. But if in the Jesuits Schools there be any Rich Burghermasters Sons who have Parts, they are sure to be snapt up, and adopted into the Society. Formerly, before the Matter was otherwise adjusted in the Dyet of *Ratisbonne*, there have been Designs of Voting Protestant Magistrates into the Government again; but so soon as the Jesuits came to discover who of the Magistrates were for that, they immediately preferred their Sons or Daughters, and made them Canons, Abbots, or Canonesses, and so diverted them by Interest. It's pity to see a City so famous for Traffick in former times, now brought to so great a decay, that were it not for the Trade of Rhenish-Wine, it would be utterly forsaken, and left wholly to the Church-Men. The continual Alarms the Magistrates have had by Foreign Designs upon their Liberty, and the Jealousies fomented among themselves, as it is thought,

thought, by the Agents and Favourers of *France*, and especially the Bishop of *Strasbourg*, have, for several years, kept them in continual disquiet, and necessitated them to raise great Taxes, which hath not a little contributed to the impoverishing of the People, especially the Boars round about; who, tho' the Country they live in be one of the most pleasant and fertile Plains of *Germany*, yet are so wretchedly poor, that Canvas Cloaths, Wooden Shoes, and Straw to sleep on in the same room with their Beasts, is the greatest worldly Happiness that most of them can attain unto. The Elector of *Cologne* is Bishop of four great Bishopricks, *viz*. Cologne, Prince of *Liege*, *Munster*, and *Heldershime*. To speak of all the Miracles of the three Kings of *Cologne*, and the vast number of Saints, who were removed out of *England* and interred there, would be but tedious, and perhaps incredible, to the Reader, as well as wide of my design: I shall therefore proceed.

FRom *Cologne* I took Water on the *Rhine*, and advanced to the City of *Bon*, and so forward to *Coblentz*, the Residence of the Elector of *Trier*: Over-against this City, on the other side of the *Rhine*, stands that impregnable Fort called *Herminshine*, built on a high rocky Hill, as high again as *Windsor-Castle*; and on the North-side of it, the River

ver *Moselle* falls into the *Rhine*, over which there is a stately Stone-Bridge. This Prince governs his Subjects as the other Spiritual Electors do, that is, both by Temporal and Spiritual Authority, which in that Country is pretty absolute. The chief Trade of this Country is in Wine, Corn, Wood and Iron.

THE next Country I came to was that of the Elector of *Mayence* or *Mentz*, who is likewise both a Secular and Ecclesiastical Prince, and governs his Subjects accordingly. He is reckoned to be wholly for the Interests of the French King; who, notwithstanding of that, pretends a Title to the Cittadel of *Mayence*. As I was upon my Journey to *Mayence* by Land, I made a turn down the *Rhine* to visit the famous little City of *Backrack*, and some Towns belonging to the Landtgrave of *Hesse*, but especially *Backrack*, because Travellers say, it much resembles *Jerusalem* in its Situation and manner of Buildings. The Burghermaster of this City told me, that the whole Country about *Backrack* does not yield above 200 Fouders of Wine a year; and yet the Merchants of *Dort*, by an Art of Multiplication, which they have used some years, furnish *England* with several thousand of Fouders. Here I shall take the Liberty to relate a strange Story, which I found recorded in this Country, tho'

MAYENCE.

I know it to be mentioned in History: There was a certain cruel and inhuman Bishop of *Mayence*, who, in a year of great scarcity and Famine, when a great number of poor People came to his Gates begging for Bread, caused the poor Wretches, Men, Women, and Children, to be put into a Barn, under pretext of relieving their Necessities, but so soon as they were got in, caused the Barn Doors to be shut, Fire set to it, and so burnt them all alive: And whilst the poor Wretches cried and shrieked out for Horror and Pain, the barbarous Miscreant said to those that were about him, Hark, how the Rats and Mice do cry. But the just Judgment of GOD suffered not the Fact to pass unpunished; for not long after the cruel Bishop was so haunted with Rats and Mice, that all the Guards he kept about him could not secure him from them, neither at Table nor in Bed; at length he resolved to flee for Safety into a Tower that stood in the middle of the *Rhine*; but the Rats pursued him, got into his Chamber, and devoured him alive; so that the Justice of the Almighty made him a Prey to Vermin, who had inhumanly reckoned his Fellow-Christians to be such. The Tower, which I saw, to this day is call'd the Rats-Tower, and the Story is upon Record in the City of *Mayence*.

On my Journey from thence I came to the little Village of *Hockim*, not far distant;

famous

famous for our Hockomore-Wine, of which, though the place does not produce above 150 Fouders a year, yet the ingenious Hollanders of *Dort* make some thousand Fouders of it go off in *England* and the *Indies*.

FRom *Hockom* I proceeded to *Francfort*, a pleasant City upon the River of *Maine*, called formerly *Teutoburgum* and *Helenopolis*, and since *Francfort*, because here the Franconians, who came out of the Province of *Franconia*, foarded over, when they went upon their Expedition into *Gallia*, which they conquered, and named it *France:* And I thought it might very well deserve the Name of *Petty-London*, because of its Privileges, and the Humour of the Citizens. It is a Hansiatick and Imperial Town, and Commonwealth, the Magistrates being Lutherans, which is the publick established Religion; though the Cathedral Church belongs to the Roman Catholicks, who also have several Monasteries there. The City is populous, and frequented by all sorts of Merchants, from most parts of *Europe*, and part of *Asia* also, because of the two great Fairs that are yearly kept there: Many Jews live in this City, and the richest Merchants are Calvinists, who are not suffered to have a Church in the Town, but half an hours Journey out of it, at a place called *Bucknam*, where I have told Seventy four Coaches at a time,

time, all belonging to Merchants of the City. It was in ancient times much enrich'd by *Charlemain*, and hath been since by the Constitution of the *Golden-Bull*: Amongst other Honours and Privileges, it's appointed to be the place of the Emperor's Election, where many of the Ornaments, belonging to that August Ceremony, are to be seen. It is strongly fortified, having a stately Stone-bridge over the *Mayne*, that joyns it to *Saxe-housen*, the Quarter of the Great Master of the Teutonick-Order. The Government is easie to the People, they not being taxed as other Cities are; and had it not been for the Alarms the French gave them, during the last War, they had not been much troubled, but being forced to keep 3 or 4000 Men in constant Pay to defend their Fortifications, the Magistrates were constrained to raise Money by a Tax. Besides that of the Emperor, they are under the Protection of some Neighbouring Princes, as of the Landtgrave of *Hesse-Cassel*, Landtgrave of *Armstadt*, the Count of *Solmes*, and the Count of *Hanau*, who are either Lutherans or Calvinists, amongst whom the late Elector *Palatine* was also one; but whether the present, who is a Roman Catholick, be so or not, I cannot tell. This City takes great care of their Poor, and in their Charity to poor Travellers exceed *Holland*: I have seen a List of Seven thousand

whom

whom they relieved in one year. Their great Hospital is a large Court or Palace, where the English Merchants formerly lived, in the time of Queen *Mary*'s Persecution of the Protestants, who, when they were recalled by Queen *Elizabeth*, were so generous as to give the whole Court, with all their Pack-houses and Lands to the Poor of the City. It was my fortune to be there in that cold Winter in the year 1683, and saw a Ceremony performed by the Wine-Coopers of the City, who are obliged by Law, that when ever the *Maine* lies fast frozen over for 8 days together, to make a great Fouder Fat, Hoops and Staves, and set it up compleat upon the Ice. It was very good diversion to see so many Hands at Work, and to observe the jollity and mirth of the many Thousands of Spectators, who wanted not plenty of Rhenish Wine to Carouse in.

I had the curiosity afterward to go to the Court of the Landtgrave of *Armestadt*, a Lutheran Prince, who lives in part of the richest Soil in *Germany*. His Highness is a very courteous and obliging Prince to Strangers, and his Subjects are in a pretty good Condition again, though they have been great Sufferers by the last War between the Landtgrave of *Hesse* and this Family.

From

HEIDELBERG.

From thence I went to *Heidleberg*, a City I had been formerly in, in the Life time of that Wife, though unfortunate Prince Elector, Elder Brother to Prince *Rupert*. Here I had the Honour to pay my Dutiful Respects to the Elector, the Son of that great Prince, whose Commissary I had the Honour to be for two years together in *Amsterdam*. This Prince, since my being there, is Dead, and left behind him the Reputation of having been a zealous thorough paced Calvinist, and so constant a frequenter of the Church, that some Sundays he went thrice a day to Sermon; but never failed, if in Health, to be once a day at least at the Garison Church, where he took particular notice of such Officers as were absent. He was Married to a most Virtuous Lady, the Royal Sister of the King of *Denmark*, and his Brother Prince *George*. During his Life time the University of *Heidleberg* flourished exceedingly, so that the number of Students was so great, that Chambers and Lodgings in the City were scarce, and *Spanhemius* was about quitting *Leyden* to return to his Professors place in *Heidleberg*; but how matters stand since his Death, I am as yet ignorant. This Country is called, the Paradise of *Germany*, for its fruitfulness in Wine, Corn, and all sorts of Fruit. I my self have seen growing in one Plain, at the same time, Vines, Corn, Chestnuts,

Cheſtnuts, Almonds, Dates, Figs, Cherries, beſides ſeveral other ſorts of Fruit. And as the Country is fertile in yielding the Fruits of the Earth, ſo the People are careful in providing Store Room for them. This I take notice of, becauſe of the prodigious Rheniſh Wine Fats which are to be ſeen there, amongſt which there are Seven, the leaſt whereof holds the quantity of 250 Barils of Beer, as I calculated; but the large and moſt celebrated Fat is that which goes by the name of the great Tun of *Heidleberg*, and holds 204 *Fouders of Wine, and coſt 705 *l.* Sterling in Building, for which one may have a very good Houſe built. This Fat I have ſeen twice, and the firſt time was, when the Elector Treated the French Ambaſſadors that came to conclude the Match betwixt his Daughter, and Monſieur the French Kings Brother, who Married her after the Death of *Henrietta* his firſt Wife; at which Treat there happened an adventure, that I ſhall here pleaſe the Reader with. In a Gallery that is over this Fat, the Elector cauſed a Table to be placed in the middle, exactly above the Bunghole of this Monſtrous Veſſel, and to be covered with a coſtly Banquet of all ſorts of Sweat-Meats: The day before, all the Wine being emptied out of this Tun into other Fats, a little before the Ambaſſadors, with other Foreign Miniſters and Perſons of Quality mounted the Stairs to come to the place of

* *A Fouder contains 4 Hogſheads.*

of Entertainment, the Elector caused twelve Drummers, with as many Trumpeters, some Kettle-Drums, and other Musick, to be lodged in the Belly of the Tun, with orders to strike up, upon a signal given, when the Elector drank the French Kings Health. All being sat down at Table, and merrily Feeding, the Elector drank the Health, and the Signal was given; whereupon the Musick began to play its part, with such a roaring and uncouth Noise out of that vast Cavity below, that the French and other Persons of Quality who were unacquainted with the design, looking upon it to be an infernal and ominous Sound, in great astonishment began to cry out, *Jesu Maria*, *The Worlds at an end*, and to shift every one for himself in so great Disorder and Confusion, that for haste to be gone they tumbled down Stairs one over another. All that the Elector could say to compose them, was either not heard, or not valued, nor could any thing satisfie and reassure them, till they saw the Actors come marching out of their Den. Had not many Persons of Quality and Travellers seen this Fat as well as my self, who know that what I say of its incredible bigness to be true, I should be afraid the Reader might think I imposed upon his Credulity.

From *Heidleberg* I went to see that impregnable Fort or Cittadel of *Manheim* alias *Frederickberg*, built by the Elector *Frederick*,

Brother

Brother to Prince *Rupert*, a Prince of as good a Head as any *Germany* afforded; who though some have too partially judged of him by his Misfortunes, yet by the wisest of the Age was accounted the *Cato* of *Germany*. The Wisest and best Men of the World have been unfortunate, which makes some to be of the Opinion, That God in his Wisdom thinks fit it should be so, lest otherwise they might attribute their Prosperity rather to the wise direction of their own Conduct, than his All-seeing Providence: And indeed, daily Experience seems to evince the Truth of this, since we see Knaves and Fools advanced to Preferment and Riches, when Men of Virtue and Parts die neglected, and poor in the Eyes of the World, though rich in the enjoyment of a contented Mind. But this is a digression which the Honour I have for the memory of that great Man hath led me into, and therefore I hope will be pardoned by the Reader. In the Cittadel of *Manheim* I saw some of the Records of that Illustrious Family, which without dispute is the most ancient of all the Secular Electors, being Elder to that of *Bavaria*, which sprung from one and the same Stock; to wit, two Emperors of *Germany*. Many Writers derive them originally from *Charlemain*, by the Line of *Pepin* King of *France*. There have been several Emperors of that Race, one King of *Denmark*, and four Kings of *Sueden*, one

one of which was King of *Norway* also, besides many great Generals of Armies in *Germany*, *Hungary*, *France*, and other Countrys. Since I can remember there were five Protestant Princes Heirs to that Electoral Dignity alive; which now by their Death is fallen to the Duke of *Newbourg*, the present Prince Elector *Palatine*, a Roman Catholick, whose Daughter is Empress of *Germany*, and another of his Daughters Married to the King of *Portugal*, a third to the King of *Spain*, and a fourth to Prince *James* of *Poland*.

BEing so near *Strasbourg*, I had the curiosity to go see what figure that Famous City now made, since it had changed its Master; for I had been thrice there before, when it flourished under the Emperors Protection, with the liberty of a Hansiatick Town: And indeed, I found it so disfigured, that had it not been for the stately Cathedral Church, and fair Streets, and Buildings, I could scarcely have known it. In the Streets and Exchange, which formerly were thronged with sober, rich, and peaceable Merchants, you meet with none hardly now but Men in Buff-Coats and Scarffs, with rabbles of Soldiers their Attendants. The Churches I confess are gayer, but not so much frequented by the Inhabitants as heretofore, seeing the Lutherans are thrust into the meanest Churches,

Churches, and most of the chief Merchants, both Lutherans and Calvinists, removed to *Holland* and *Hambourg*. Within a few years, I beleive it will be just such another City for Trade and Riches as *Brisac* is. It was formerly a rich City, and well stockt with Merchants and wealthy Inhabitants, who lived under a gentle and easie Government; but now the Magistrates have little else to do in the Government, but only to take their Rules and Measures from a Cittadel and great Guns, which are Edicts that Merchants least understand. I confess, *Strasbourg* is the less to be pittied that it so tamely became a Slave, and put on its Chains without any strugling. Those Magistrates who were Instruments in it, are now sensible of their own Folly, and bite their Nails for Anger, finding themselves no better, but rather worse hated than the other Magistrates, who did what they could to hinder the Reception of their new Masters the French. I quickly grew weary of being here, meeting with nothing but complaints of Poverty, and paying exorbitant Taxes.

I therefore soon returned to my *Petty-London*, *Francfort*, and from thence went to *Cassel*, the chief Residence of the Landtgrave of *Hesse*. This Prince is a Calvinist, as most of his Subjects are, very grave and zealous in his Religion: He Married a Princess of
Courland,

HESSE.

Courland, by whom he hath an hopeful Issue; to wit, three Sons, and two Daughters. King *Charles* II. was God-Father to one of his Sons, who was Christened by the Name of *Charles*; Captain *William Legg*, Brother to the Lord *Dartmouth*, representing his Majesty as his Envoy. The Court of this Prince does indeed resemble a well-governed College, or Religious Cloister, in regard of its Modesty and Regularity in all Things, and especially in the Hours of Devotion. He is Rich in Money, and entertains about Nine Thousand Men in constant Pay, under the Command of Count *Vanderlip*, a brave and expert Soldier, his Lieutenant General, but can bring many more upon occasion into Field. This Family hath been very happy both in its Progeny and Alliances, many Wise Princes of both Sexes having sprung from it; and the Mother of this present Landtgrave may be reckoned amongst the Illustrious Women of the present and past Ages. After the Death of *William* V. Landtgrave of *Hesse* her Husband, she not only supported, but advanced the War wherein he was engaged, did many signal Actions, enlarged her Territories, and at the conclusion of the Peace, kept under her Pay 56 Cornets of Horse in five Regiments, 166 Companies of Foot, besides 13 Companies of Dragoons, and 14 Independent Companies, in all 249 Companies of Horse and Foot:

Foot: She was a Princess extreamly obliging to Strangers, especially virtuous and learned Divines. I had the Honour a good many years ago to kiss her Highnesses Hand, at which time she was mighty Zealous in promoting an Accommodation amongst different Religions, as the Roman Catholick, Lutheran and Calvinist, but especially betwixt the two latter; and therefore entertained Doctor *Duris*, at her Court in *Cassels*, who wrote several pieces upon that Subject of Reconciliation, and with some of his Friends had a Conference with a Learned Priest, that came from *Rome* to forward the Project; whereupon the Doctor Published his Book of the *Harmony of Consent*, which is highly esteemed in *Germany*.

FRom this Princes Court I directed my Journey to *Hanouer*, taking *Lambspring* in my way, a place where there is a Convent of English Monks; and there I met with a very aged, worthy, and harmless Gentleman, Sir *Thomas Gascoigne*, a Person of seeming great Integrity and Piety; the Lord Abbot and several of the Monks I had seen there formerly. This Monastery is very obliging to all Strangers that Travel that way, as well as to their own Country-men, and is highly respected by the Neighbouring Princes of all Perswasions, as the Princes of the House of *Lunenburg*, the Landtgrave of *Hesse*, and Elector

HANOVER.

Elector of *Cologne*, who as Bishop of *Hilderſheim* is their Ordinary. The Town of *Lambſpring* is Lutheran, though under the Government of the Lord Abbot and his Chapter, who conſtantly chuſe Lutheran Magiſtrates and Officers for the Civil Adminiſtration, and live together in that Love and Unity, that as yet there hath never the leaſt debate happened amongſt them; and indeed, this Harmony is now to be obſerved in moſt parts of *Germany*, where different Religions are profeſſed. When I conſidered ſo many goodly Faces, both of Monks and Students in that Abbey, I could not forbear to make a ſerious Reflection on the number of the Engliſh whom I had ſeen in the Colleges and Cloiſters abroad, as at *Rome*, *Ratiſbonne*, *Wirtzburg* in *Lorrain*, at *Liege*, *Louvain*, *Bruſſels*, *Dunkirk*, *Ghent*, *Paris*, and other places, beſides the Nunneries; and withall, on the loſs that both King and Kingdom ſuffered thereby, when ſo many of our Natives, both Men and Women ſhould be conſtrained to ſpend their own Eſtates, and the Benevolence of others in a ſtrange Land, which amounts to more Money than at firſt one may imagine; and this thought, I confeſs, made me wiſh it were otherwiſe. I would not have the Reader to miſtake me here, as if I Eſpouſed, or Pleaded for any particular Party; no, I plead only for the Sentiments of Humanity, without which our Nature degenerates into that of Brutes, and for the love that every honest Man ought to have for his Country. I am as much a Friend to the Spanish Inquisition, as to the persecuting of tender Conscienced Protestants, provided there be no more but Conscience in the Case: And I could heartily wish that Papists and Protestants could live as lovingly together in *England*, as they do in *Holland*, *Germany*, and other Countries; for give me leave to say it, I love not that Religion, which in stead of Exalting, destroys the Principles of Morality and human Society. I have met with honest Men of all Perswasions, even Turks and Jews, who in their Lives and Manners have far exceeded many of our Enthusiastick Professors at home; and when ever this happened, I could not forbear to love the Men without embracing their Religion, for which they themselves are to account to their great Master and Judge.

In my progress towards *Hanouer* I touched at *Hilderfheim*, a City whose Magistrates are Lutheran, though Roman Catholicks have the Cathedral Church, and several Monasteries there. The Court of *Hanouer* makes another kind of Figure than that of *Caffels*, it being the Court of a greater Prince, who is Bishop of *Ofnaburg*, Duke of *Brunfwick*, *Lunenburg*, *Hanouer*, &c. Here I had the Honour to Kiss the

hands

HANOVER.

Hands of the Princess Royal *Sophia*, youngest Sister to the late Prince *Rupert*. Her Highness has the Character of the *Merry Debonnaire* Princess of *Germany*, a Lady of Extraordinary Virtue and Accomplishments, and Mistress of the Italian, French, High and Low Dutch, and English Languages, which she speaks to Perfection. Her Husband has the Title of the Gentleman of *Germany*, a graceful and comely Prince both a Foot, and on Horseback, Civil to Strangers beyond compare, infinitely Kind and Beneficent to People in Distress, and known in the World for a Valiant and Experienced Soldier. I had the Honour to see his Troops, which, without Controversie are as good Men, and Commanded by as expert Officers as any are in *Europe*: Amongst his Officers I found brave *Steel-Hand Gordon*, Colonel of an excellent Regiment of Horse, *Grimes*, *Hamilton*, *Talbot*, and others of our Kings Subjects. God hath blest the Prince with a numerous Off-spring, having six Sons, all gallant Princes; of whom the two Eldest signalized themselves so bravely at the raising of the Siege of *Vienna*, that as undoubted proof of their Valour, they brought three Turks home to this Court Prisoners. His eldest Son is Married to a most beautiful Princess, sole Heiress of the Duke of *Lunenburg* and *Zell's* Elder Brother; as the lovely Princess his

Daughter

Daughter is Married to the Duke of *Brandenburg*. He is a gracious Prince to his People, and keeps a very splendid Court, having in his Stables for the use of himself and Children, no less than Fifty two sets of Coach-Horses: He himself is a Lutheran, but as his Subjects are Christians of different Perswasions, and some of them Jews too, so both in his Court and Army he entertains Gentlemen of various Opinions and Countries, as *Italian* Abbots, and Gentlemen that serve him, and many Calvinist French Officers: Neither is he so Bigotted in his Religion, but that he and his Children go many times to Church with the Princess, who is a Calvinist, and join with her in her Devotion. His Country is good, having Gold and Silver Mines in it, and his Subjects live well under him; as do those also of his Brother the Duke of *Lunenburg*, and their Cozen the Duke of *Wolfembuttel*, which are the three Princes of the House of *Lunenburg*; of whom it may be said, that they have always stuck honestly to the right side, and befriended the Interests of the Empire; so that no by-Respect, neither Honour nor Profit, could ever prevail with them, as it has with others, to make them abandon the publick Concern.

From

FRom this Princes Court I went to *Zell*, the Residence of the Duke the elder Brother of the Family. This Prince is called the Mighty *Nimrod*, because of the great delight he takes in Horses, Dogs, and Hunting. He did me the honour to let me see his Stables, wherein he keeps 370 Horses, most of them English, or of English Breed. His Dogs, which are also English, are so many, that with great care they are quartered in several Apartments according to their Kind and Qualities, there being a large Office like a Brewhouse employed for boyling of Malt and Corn for them. It is this valiant Prince who took *Trieves* from the French, and made the Mareschal *de Crequi* Prisoner: He is extreamly obliging to Strangers, and hath several brave Scotish Officers under his Pay, as Major-General *Erskin*, *Graham*, *Coleman*, *Hamilton*, *Melvin*, and others. His Lieutenant-General is one *Chavot* a Protestant of *Alsatia*, an excellent and experienced Commander. I shall add no more concerning this Prince, his Officers, or Country; but that he, with the other two Princes of the House of *Lunenbourg*, *Hanouer*, and *Wolfembuttel*, can upon occasion bring into the Field 36000 Soldiers, whom they keep in constant Pay; and such Men as I never saw better in my life.

After some stay at the Court of the Duke of *Zell*, I went to *Hambourg*, a famous Hanfiatick Town. It is a Republick, and City of great Trade, occasioned partly by the English Company of *Merchant Adventurers*, but much more by the Dutch Proteftants, who in the time of the Duke of *Alba* forfook the Low-Countries and fettled here, and the Proteftants alfo who were turned out of *Cologne*, and other Places in *Germany*; who neverthelefs are not now allowed Publick Churches within the City, but at a place called *Altena*, a Village belonging to the King of *Denmark*, a quarter of an hours walk diftant from *Hambourg*. This Commonwealth is *Lutheran*, and governed by 4 Burghermafters, 24 Radts-heers, and a Common-Council of all the Burghers who have above 40 Shillings per *Annum* Freehold. The Symbol or Motto under their Arms, is, *Da Pacem Domine in Diebus noftris*; and in their Standards are thefe Letters *S. P. Q. H.* The People here groan under heavy Taxes and Impofitions; The State, becaufe of continual Alarms they have from the King of *Denmark*, or other Neighbours; and the Inteftine Broils that frequently happen here, as well as at *Cologne*, where the Burghermafters are often in danger of their Lives from the mutinous Mobile; being forced to maintain 6 or 7000 Men in Pay, befides 2 or 3 Men of War to guard

guard their Havens from Pirats. I shall not name all the ways of imposing Taxes which this Commonwealth uses, because in most they imitate the Methods of the States-General as to that, which have been mentioned before: I shall only take notice of some peculiar Customs they have, wherein they differ from *Holland*. When a Barber, Shoemaker, or any other Artizan dies, leaving a Widow and Children, another of the same Trade is not admitted to set up for himself as a Master, unless he compound with the Widow for a piece of Money, or else marry her, or a Daughter of hers with her consent.

If any Man cause another to be Arrested for Debt, or upon any other Suit, the Plaintiff must go along with the Officer who Arrests the Party, and stay by him until the Prisoner be examined by the Sheriff; so that if the Sheriff be not to be spoken with that night, the Plaintiff must tarry with the Prisoner all night, until the Sheriff examin the matter, and see cause of discharging or committing the Party; but this a Plaintiff may do by a Procuration Notarial.

If a Prisoner be committed for Debt, the Plaintiff must maintain him in Prison according to his Quality; and if the Party lie in Prison during the space of 6 Years, at the expiration of that time the Prisoner is dis-

discharged; and if during the time of his Imprisonment the Plaintiff do not punctually pay the Prisoner's Allowance at the Months end, the Prisoner is set at liberty, and nevertheless the Plaintiff must pay the Gaoler the last Month's Allowance.

This State is severe in the execution of Justice against Thieves, Murderers, and Cheats. There is no Pardon to be expected for Murder, and a Burghermaster himself, if Guilty, cannot escape. The Punishment for Murder is here as in *Sweden*, breaking Malefactors on the Wheel, pinching their Breasts and Arms with hot Pincers, spitting them in at the Fundament, and out at the Shoulder: They have also cruel ways of Torturing to make Prisoners confess; and are very careful not to be cheated in their Publick Revenue, their Excise-men and Collectors being Punished as in *Holland*. They take a very good course not to be cheated in their Excise, for all the Mills of the Country are in the hands of the State; so that no Baker nor Brewer can grind his own Corn, but must have it ground at the States Mills, where they pay the Excise. There is a General Tax upon all Houses, and that is the Eighth Penny, which nevertheless does not excuse them from Chimney-money. The States here, as at *Genoua* in *Italy*, are the Publick Vintners, of whom all People must buy their Wine, which they

they buy from the Merchant, or otherwise import it in their own Ships. In their Ceremonies of Burying and Christening, they are ridiculously Prodigal; as for Instance: If one invite a Burghermaster, he must give him a Ducat in Gold; if a Radts-heer, that is, an Alderman, a Rixdollar; to every Preacher, Doctor of Physick, Advocate or Secretary, half a Rixdollar; and to every Schoolmaster, the third part of a Rixdollar. The Women are the Inviters to Burials, Weddings, and Christenings, who wear an Antick kind of a Dress, having Mitred Caps as high again as the Mitre of a Bishop. The Churches here are rich in Revenues and Ornaments, as Images and stately Organs, wherein they much delight. They are great Lovers of *Musick*, insomuch that I have told 75 Masters of several sorts of Musick in one Church, besides those who were in the Organ-Gallery. Their Organs are extraordinary large: I measured the great Pipes in the Organs of St. *Catherine*'s and St. *James*'s Churches, and found them to be 3 Foot and 3 quarters in circumference, and 32 Foot long; in each of which Organs there are two Pipes 5 Foot and 8 Inches round. The Wealth and Trade of this City encreases daily; they send one Year with another 70 Ships to *Greenland*, and have wonderfully Ingrossed that Trade from *England* and *Holland*, and it's believed, that

that small and great there are belonging to this Commonwealth five thousand Sail of Ships. After *Amsterdam, Genoua* and *Venice*, their Bank is reckoned the chief in Credit; but in Trade they are accounted the third in *Europe*, and come next to *London* and *Amsterdam*. *Hamburg* is now become the Magazine of *Germany*, and of the Baltick and Northern Seas. They give great Privileges to the Jews, and to all Strangers whatsoever, especially the English Company of Merchant Adventurers, whom they allow a large Building, where they have a Church, and where the Deputy-Governour, Secretary, Minister, and the other Officers of the Company live, to whom they yearly make Presents of Wine, Beer, Sheep, Salmond and Sturgeon in their seasons. And so much of *Hambourg*.

From *Hambourg* I went to *Lubeck*, which is also a Commonwealth and Imperial Town. It is a large well-built City, containing ten Parish-Churches; the Cathedral dedicated to St. *Peter* being in length 500 Foot, with two high Spires all covered with Brass, as the rest of the Churches of that City are. In former times this City was the place where the Deputies of all the Hansiatick Towns assembled, and was once so powerful as to make War against *Denmark* and *Sweden*, and to conquer several places and Islands belonging to those two Crowns, nay

nay and to lend Ships to *England* and other Potentates, without any prejudice to their own Trade, wherein they vyed in all parts with their Neighbours; but it is now exceedingly run into decay, not only in Territories, but in Wealth and Trade also. And the reason of that was chiefly the Inconsiderate Zeal of their Lutheran Ministers, who perswaded the Magistrates to banish all Roman Catholicks, Calvinists, Jews, and all that dissented from them in matter of Religion, even the English Company too, who all went and setled in *Hambourg*, to the great Advantage of that City, and almost ruine of *Lubeck*, which hath not now above 200 Ships belonging to it, nor more Territories to the State than the City it self, and a small part called *Termond*, about eight Miles distant from it. The rest of their Territories are now in the possession of the Danes and Swedes, by whom the Burghers are so continually alarmed, that they are quite tired out with keeping Guard, and paying of Taxes. The City is indeed well fortified; but the Government not being able to maintain above 1500 Soldiers in pay, 400 Burghers in two Companies are obliged to watch every Day. They have a large well-built Stadthouse, and an Exchange covered, on the top whereof the Globes of the World are painted. This Exchange is about 50 Yards in the length, and but 15 in breadth: Over it there is a Room where

where the Skins of five Lyons which the Burghers killed at the City-Gates in the Year 1252. are kept stuft. The great Market-place is very large, where a Monumental-Stone is to be seen, on which one of their Burghermasters was beheaded for running away without fighting in a Sea-Engagement. The People here spend much time in their Churches at Devotion, which consists chiefly in Singing. The Women are beautiful, but disfigured with a kind of Antick Dress, they wearing Cloaks like Men. It is cheap living in this Town: For one may hire a Palace for a matter of 20 *l.* a Year, and have Provisions at very reasonable Rates; besides the Air and Water is very good, the City being supplied with Fountains of Excellent Fresh Water, which *Hambourg* wants; and good Ground for Celleridge, there being Cellars here 40 or 50 Foot deep.

I Had the Curiosity to go from *Lubeck* to see the Ancient City of *Magdeburg*, but found it so ruined and decayed by the Swedish War, that I had no Encouragement to stay there. I therefore hastened to *Berlin*, the chief Residence of the Elector of *Brandenburg*; at whose Court I met with a very Ingenuous French Merchant, who told me, that he, and divers other Merchants, were designed to have lived in *England*, but were discouraged by a Letter sent from *London*, by a French-Man that was removing from thence to *Amsterdam*, for these following Reasons, which I Copied out of his Letter.

First, Because the Reformed Religion is persecuted in *England* as it is *France*; the which I told him was a great Untruth, for it is apparent that they have been all along graciously admitted, and received into his Majesties Dominions, without interruption, and allowed the free Exercise of their own Form of Worship, according to the Doctrine and Discipline of the Churches of *France*. Nor can they who converse with the French Ministers either in *France* or *Holland* be ignorant, that the chiefest part, if not all those Ministers, are willing to comply with the Church of *England*; and it is evident that most of the Dutch and French Protestants (so called) in *Holland* make use of Organs in their Churches.

A second thing was, that both the Bank at *London* and the Bankers Goldsmiths were all broak; the which I told this Frenchman was not true altogether, for there are many able Bankers whom I named: Neither was the Bank (as he called the Chamber of *London*) broak, only it had been under the management of a bad Person, whose design was to bring it into disgrace. Besides, there is the *East-India Company* an unquestionable Security for those as have Money to dispose of, together with another undeniable Security which is Land. Third-

Thirdly, he saith, That in *England* there is no Register, and therefore many Frauds in Purchases and Morgages, which beget tedious Suits, and renders both dangerous to trust.

Fourthly, That if a Man would purchase Land he cannot, being an Alien, until Naturalized.

Fifthly, That in *England* there are so many Plots and Confusions in Government, that the Kingdom is hardly quiet 20 Years together.

Sixthly, that false Witnesses were so common in *England*, and the Crime of Perjury so slightly punished, that no Man could be safe in Life or Estate, if he chanced to be in Trouble.

Lastly he said, that the English are so restless and quarelsom, that they not only foment and cherish Animosities amongst one another, but are every foot contriving and plotting against their Lawful Sovereign, and the Government. By such Surmises and Insinuations as these, the French and Germans are scared from trusting themselves and Fortunes in *England*, and therefore settle in *Amsterdam*, *Hamburgh*, and other Cities, where there are Banks and Registers: This I say is one cause, why there are now to be seen at *Amsterdam* such vast numbers of French and Germans, who have much enrich'd that City, and raised the Rents of the Houses 20

for

per Cent. And the Silk-weavers grow also very rich, keeping so-many Alms-Children to do their Work, and having all their Labour without any Charge, only for the teaching them their Trades; which hath lessened the Revenues of the French Crown, and will, in time, greatly increase the number of the States Subjects, and advance their publick Incomes.

Having made this Digression, I return to *Berlin*; It is a City enlarged with fair Streets and Palaces: The Magistrates of the place are Lutherans, which is the publick established Religion in all the Electors Dominions; though he himself and his Children be Calvinists: He is look'd upon to be so true to that Persuasion, that he is reckoned the Protector of the Calvinists; and indeed he sollicited the Emperor very hard for a Toleration of the Protestants in *Hungary*. His Chaplains, as most of the Lutheran Ministers also, endeavour to imitate the English in their way of Preaching: And his Highness is so much taken with English Divinity, that he entertains Divines for translating English Books into the German Tongue, as *The Whole Duty of Man*, and several others. He has a large and stately Palace at *Berlin*, and therein a copious Library, enriched with many Manuscripts, Medals, and Rarities of Antiquity. He may compare with most Princes for handsom Guards, being all of them

them proper well-bodied Men, and moſt part Officers who ride in his Guards of Horſe. As he is known in the World to be a Valiant and Warlike Prince, ſo he maintains in Pay an Army of 36000 Men; beſides five or ſix thouſand Horſemen, who in time of War are modelled into Troops; with which Body during the late War with *Sweden*, his Highneſs's Father in Perſon beat the *Swedes* out of his Country. He keeps his Forces in ſtrict Diſcipline, obliging all the Officers, if Proteſtants, on *Sundays* and Holy-days to march their ſeveral Companies in order to Church; but if a Superiour Officer be of a contrary Perſwaſion, then the next in Commiſſion ſupplies his place. This cuſtom is Religiouſly obſerved by all his Highneſſes Gariſons, whilſt he himſelf goes conſtantly to the Calviniſt Church adjoyning to the Court, with his Children, being five Sons, two Daughters, and two Daughters-in-Law.

Amongſt other Acts of Publick Piety and Charity, this Prince hath eſtabliſhed and endowed ſome Religious Houſes or Nunneries for Proteſtant young Ladies, where they may live virtuouſly, and ſpend their time in Devotion as long as they pleaſe, or otherwiſe Marry; if they think fit, but then they loſe the benefit of the Monaſtery. There is one of theſe at *Hertford* in *Weſtphalia*, where I was, and had the Honour to wait upon

the

the Lady Abbess the Princess *Elizabeth*, eldest Sister of the late Elector Palatine and Prince *Rupert*. Notwithstanding the late Wars with *Sweden*, and that by the prevalency of *France* in that hasty Treaty of Peace concluded at *Nimeguen*, his late Electoral Highness was obliged to give back what he had justly taken from that Crown; yet his Subjects flourished in Wealth and Trade, his Highness having encouraged Manufactures of all sorts, by inviting Artizans into his Dominions, and established a Company of Trading Merchants to the *West-Indies*, which will much advance Navigation amongst his Subjects. And in all humane probability they are like to continue in a happy condition, seeing by the Alliances his Highness hath made with the Protestant Princes of the Empire, and especially the House of *Lunenbourg*, they are in no danger of being disturbed by their Neighbours.

I told you before that the Elector of *Brandenbourg* was Married to the Daughter of the Duke of *Hanouer*, so that as long as that Alliance holds, the Families of *Brandenbourg* and *Lunenbourg* will be in a condition to cast the Balance of the Empire; they both together being able to bring into the Field 80000 as good Men as any are in *Europe*.

WHen I parted from *Berlin*, I made a turn back to *Lunenbourg* in my way to *Swedeland*, where I found several of my Countrymen Officers in the Garison, who shewed me what was most remarkable in the City, as the Saltworks, (which bring in considerable Sums of Money to the Duke of *Lunenbourg*) the Stadthouse, and Churches, in one of which I saw a Communion-Table of pure Ducat-Gold. From thence I went into the Province of *Holstein*, and at a small Sea-port called *Termond*, of which I spake before, I embarked for *Sweden*.

STOCKHOLM.

HE that hath read in the Histories of this last Age the great Exploits of *Gustavus Adolphus* and his *Swedes*, perhaps may have a fancy that it must be an excellent Country which hath bred such Warriors; but if he approach it, he will soon find himself undeceived. Entering into *Swedeland*, at a place called *Landsort*, we sail'd forward amongst high Rocks, having no other prospect from Land but Mountains till we came to *Dollers*, which is about four Swedish, that is, twenty four English Miles from *Stockholm*, the Capital City of the Kingdom. Upon my coming ashore, I confess I was a little surprized to see the Poverty of the People; and the little Wooden Houses they lived in, not unlike Soldiers Huts in a Leaguer; but much more, when I discovered little else in the Country but Mountainous Rocks, and standing Lakes of Water. The Reader will excuse me, I hope, if I remark not all that I may have taken notice of in this Country, seeing by what I have already written, he may perceive that my Design is rather to observe the Manner of the Inhabitants living, than to give a full Description of every thing that may be seen in the Country they live in. However, I shall say somewhat of that too, having premised once for all, that the ordinary People are wretchedly poor; yet not so much occasioned by the Publick Taxes, as as the Barronness of their Country, and the Oppression of the Nobles their Landlords, and immediate Superiours, who till the present King put a stop to their Violences, tyrannically domineered over the Lives and Fortunes of the poor Peasants.

From *Dellers* I took Waggon to *Stockholm*, changing Horses three times by the way, by reason of the badness of the Rode, on all hands environed with Rocks, that hardly open so much as here and there to leave a shred of plain Ground. At two Miles distance upon that Road the City of *Stockholm* looks great, because of the King's Palace, the Houses of Noblemen, and some Churches which are seated upon Rocks: And indeed, the whole City and Suburbs stand upon Rocks, unless it be some few Houses built upon Ground gained from the Rivers that run through the Town. *Stockholm* has its Name from a Stock or Log of Wood, which three Brothers threw into the Water five Miles above the City, making a Vow, that where-ever that Stock should stop, they would build a Castle to dwell in. The Stock stopt at the Holm, or Rock where the Palace of the King now stands: And the Brothers, to be as good as their word, there built their Castle, which invited others to do the like; so that in process of time the other Rocks or Holms were covered with Buildings, which at length became the Capital City

City of the Kingdom. It is now embellished with a great many stately Houses, and much improved from what it was 400 Years ago, as indeed most Cities are; for the Stadthouse then built, is so contemptible and low, that in *Holland* or *England* it would not be suffered to stand to disgrace the Nation. The Council-Chamber where the Burghmasters and Raedt sit, is two Rooms cast into one, not above nine Foot high; and the two Rooms where the Sheriffs and the Erve College (which is a Judicature like to the Doctors Commons in *England*) sit, are not above eight Foot and a half high. The King's Palace is a large Square of Stone-building, in some places very high, but an old and irregular Fabrick, without a sufficient quantity of Ground about it for Gardens and Walks. It was anciently surrounded with Water; but some Years since part of it was filled up to make a Way from the Castle-Gate down into the old Town. In this Palace there are large Rooms; but the Lodgings of the King, Queen, and Royal Family, are three Pair of Stairs high, the Rooms in the first and second Stories being destin'd for the Senate-Chamber, and other Courts of Judicature. The King's Library is four Pair of Stairs high, being a Room about forty six Foot square, with a Closet adjoyning to it not half the Dimensions. When I considered the Apartments and Furniture of this Court,

I began to think that the French Author wrote Truth, who in his Remarks upon *Swedeland* says, That when Queen *Christina* resigned the Crown to *Carolus Gustavus*, the Father of this present King, she disposed of the best of the Furniture of the Court, and gave away a large share of the Crown-Lands to her Favorites; in so much that the King, considering the poor Condition she had left the Kingdom in, and seeing the Court so meanly furnished, said, That had he known before he accepted the Crown, what then he did, he would have taken other Measures.

There are many other stately Palaces in *Stockholm* belonging to the Nobility; but many of them for want of Repairs, and not being inhabited, run to ruine; several of the Nobles who lived in them formerly, having lost the Estates that maintained their ancient Splendor, as we shall see hereafter, being retired unto a Country Life. There are also some other Magnificent Structures begun, but not finished, as that stately Building intended for a Parliament-House for the Nobles, and two or three Churches: But what I most wonder at, is the Vault wherein the late King lies buried, is not as yet covered but with Boards, for it is to be observed that the Kings of *Sweden* have no Tombs and Monuments as in *England* and other Countries; but are put into Copper Coffins, with Inscriptions

scriptions on them, and placed one by another in Vaults, adjoyning to the Gray-Friers Church. These Vaults are about eight in Number, having Turrets over them, with Veins of Copper gilt, carved into the Cyphers of the several Kings who give them their Names by being the first that are interred in them. The Vault of the late King is not yet finished, no more than the Fabricks above-mentioned, which perhaps may be imputed to the late Troubles of *Swedeland*. The Number of the Inhabitants of *Stockholm* are also much decreased within these few Years, partly by reason of the removal of the Court of Admiralty and the Kings Ships from that City to *Charles-Crown*, a new Haven lately made about 200 English Miles from thence, which hath drawn many Families belonging to the Fleet and Admiralty from *Stockholm* to live there: And partly, because many of the Nobility, Gentry, and those that depended on them, are, as I said before, withdrawn from *Stockholm* to a retired Life in the Country. Nevertheless the ordinary sort of Burghers, who still remain, are extreamly poor; seeing the Women are fain to work like Horses, drawing Carts, and as Labourers in *England*, serving Masons and Bricklayers with Stone, Bricks and Mortar, and unloading Vessels that bring those Materials; some of the poor Creatures in the Summer-time toiling in their Smocks with-

out

out either Shooes or Stockings. They perform also the part of Watermen, and for a small matter will Row Passengers 40 Miles or more if they please.

The Court here is very thin and silent, the King living frugally, and seldom Dining in publick. He Eats commonly with the two Queens, his Mother and Consort, who is a Virtuous Princess, Sister to the King of *Denmark*. She is the Mother of five Children, three Sons and two Daughters, with whom she spends most of her time in Retirement. The King is a goodly Prince, whom God hath Blessed and Endowed with Accomplishments far beyond what might have been expected from his Education, wherein he was extreamly abused, being Taught little more than his Mother Tongue. He is Gracious, Just and Valiant, constant at his Devotion, and utterly averse from all kind of Debauchery, and the unfashionable Vanities of other Courts, in Plays and Dancing.

His sports are Hunting and Exercising of his Guards, and he rarely appears publickly, or gives Audience to Strangers, which is imputed to his Sense of the neglect of his Education. He is a Prince that hath had a very hard beginning in the World, which hath many times proved fortunate to great Men; and indeed, if we consider all the circumstances of his early Misfortunes, how

he

he was slighted and neglected by his Nobles, who would hardly vouchsafe to pay him a visit when he was among them in the Country, or to do him Homage for the Lands they held of the Crown; and how by the pernicious Counsels of the French, and the weakness or treachery of his Governors, he was misled into a War that almost cost him his Crown, having lost the best of his Territories in *Germany* and *Schonen*, and most of his Forces both by Sea and Land: If, I say, these things be considered, it will probably appear, that hardly any Prince before him hath in a shorter time, or more fully setled the Authority and Prerogative of the Crown, than he hath done in *Sweden*; for which he stands no ways obliged to *France*, as he was for the Restauration of what he lost during the War. He is now as absolute as the French King, and makes Edicts, which have the Force of Laws, without the concurrence of the Estates of the Kingdom. He hath erected two Judicatures, the one called the College of Reduction, and the other of Inspections; the first of which hath put his Majesty in Possession again of all Lands alienated from the Crown, and the other called to account all Persons, even the Heirs and Executors of those who had cheated the Crown, and made them refund what they or their Predecessors had appropriated to their own use of

the

the publick Revenue. These two necessary Constitutions, as they have reduced many great Families to a pinch, who formerly lived splendidly upon the Crown Lands and Revenues, and obliged them to live at home upon their ancient and private Patrimony in the Country, which is one great cause that the Court of *Sweden* is at present so unfrequented; so have they enabled his Majesty, without burdening of his Subjects, to support the Charges of the Government, and to maintain 64000 Men in pay. The Truth is, his other Revenues are but small, what arises from the Copper and Iron Mines, one Silver Mine, the Pitch and Tar, the Customs and Excise amounts to no extraordinary Sum of Money, and the Land Tax in so barren a Country scarcely deserving to be named. The Customes and Excise, I confess, are very high, and the rigorous manner of exacting them pernicious to Trade: As for instance; If a Ship come to *Stockholme* from *London*, with a hunderd several sorts of Goods, and those Goods assigned to fifty several Men more or less, if any of those fifty do not pay the Custom of what belongs to him, though it be for a Barrel of Beer, the Ship shall not be unladen, nor no Man have his Goods out, though he hath fully pay'd the Customs for them, till this last Man hath pay'd his. There are several other silly

Customs

STOCKHOLM. 125

Customs in *Swedeland* that discourages Men from Trading there; as if any Stranger Die there, a third of his Estate must go to the City or Town where he Traded. No Foreign Merchant in *Stockholme* can Travel into any Country where there is a Fair without a Passport: And at present, seeing there is no Treaty of Trade betwixt *England* and *Sweden*, though the English bring as considerable a Trade to that Kingdom as any other Country whatsoever, yet they are very unkindly used by the Officers of the Custom-House; whereas the Dutch in *Lubeck*, and other Cities, have new and greater Privileges allowed them. Nor would I Counsel an English-man to go to Law with a Swedish Burgher in *Sweden*, especially if he be a Whiggish Scot, who hath got his Freedom in *Stockholme*, for those are a kind of Scrapers, whom I have observed to be more inveterate against the English than the Native Swedes.

Of all the Swedish Army of 64000 Men, the King keeps but 12 Companies of 200 Men a-peice, with some few Horse Guards in *Stockholme*, who are not upon Duty as Sentinels at the Court Gates, as at the Courts of other Princes. The rest are dispersed into Quarters and Garisons upon the Frontiers, which are so far distant in that large compass of Land which his Territories take up, that it would require a hard and tedious work to bring them together to a general Muster.

They

They are however kept under very strict Discipline, and those that lie near, often viewed by the King. They have odd sorts of Punishments for the Soldiers and Officers of all Degrees: For Example, if a Serjeant or Corporal be Drunk, or negligent on Duty, they are put into Armour, and with three Muskets tied under each Arm, made to walk two Hours before the Court of Guard; yet, for all the severity of Discipline used against the Soldiers, they commit many Abuses in the Night time, Robbing, and sometimes killing Men upon the Streets in *Stockholme*, where they have no Lights nor Guards as in *Copenhagen*. In former times there have been at one time 35 Colonels, besides General Officers in the Swedish Army, all the Subjects of the King of *Great Britain*, but at present there are few or none, unless it be the Sons of some Scotish Officers Deceased; nor did I ever see an English-Man in the Kings Guards, Horse or Foot, but one, and the Son of Sir *Edward Wood*, who hath since quitted the Service. The King hath exceedingly won the Hearts of the common People, not only by exempting them from the Tyrannical Jurisdiction of the Nobility and Gentry, who formerly would by their own private Authority, punish and put to Death the Peasants at their pleasure, which makes the Countries very willing to Quarter the Kings Soldiers, but by his exactness

ness in punishing Duels, Murder, and Robberies. Perjury is Death here also, as in *Holland*, which makes the Magistrates in some parts of this Kings Territories, enjoyn strange kinds of Oaths to deter Men from being forsworn: As for instance, in some places the Witness is set with a Staff in his Hand upon some Peeble Stones and Charcoal, where he is to imprecate and pray, that if what he Sweareth be not true, his Land may become as barren as those Stones, and his Substance be Consumed to Ashes like the Coals he stands on, which as soon as he steps down are set on Fire. This manner of Swearing so terrifies the People, that they commonly tremble when they come to take their Oath.

The Religion of the Dominions of the King of *Sweden*, as of those of the King of *Denmark*, and of other Princes and States whom we have named, is Lutheran, who are more rigid to Roman Catholicks and Calvinists than the Protestants of *Germany*. There is no Toleration allowed here to Calvinist Ministers; and they take an effectual course to keep the Country clear of Priests and Jesuits, by Guelding them, whether they be young or old. In Commemoration of the great Losses and Desolation sustained in the late War, the Suedes strictly keep four Fasting Days in the Months of *April*, *May*, *June*, and *July*; on which days all Men are prohibited by Authority to kindle Fire in their Houses,

Houses, or to Eat till after Evening Service is done, which in the Winter time could not be endured. They delight much in Singing in their Churches, which they constantly perform twice every day, Morning and Evening. In their Marryings, Christenings, and Buryings they are so prodigally extravagant, that if all three happen in one year to a Man of a competent Estate, it is enough to break him. The Clergy of *Sweden* are neither so Rich nor Learned as those of *Germany*, wanting both the opportunities of Study, and of conversing with Learned Men, that those of other Countrys enjoy, though there be some Learned Men amongst them. A Bishoprick in *Sweden* is no great Benefice, if compared with some Parsonages in *England*; for the Arch-bishop, and Metropolitan hath not above 400 *l. per Annum*, and some of the rest are not worth above 150 or 200 *l.* a year. The inferiour Clergy are not so regular in their Lives and Conversation in the Countries distant from *Stockholme*, as they are near the Court; and the Reason is, partly because they entertain Travellers that pass the Country, there being no Inns in most places for the Accommodation of Persons of any Quality, and so are obliged to drink with their Guests; and partly, because at Buryings and Christenings, where there is commonly high Drinking, the Pape or Parson is Master of the Ceremonies: And here give me leave

to

to tell a short Story of one of them. A Pape coming to Christen a Child in a Church, and finding a Scotch Man to be Godfather, was so transported either with Zeal, or his Cups, that when he came to exorcise the Child, which is a Rite used in their Office of Administring this Sacrament; he neglected the Form prescribed by the Liturgy, and in an extemporary Prayer begg'd, that the Devil might depart out of the Child, and enter into that Scottish Heretick, for so they call the Presbyterians of that Nation. The Prayer of the Pape so incensed the Scot, that he vowed Revenge, and watched the Pape with a good Cudgel next day as he crossed the Church-yard, where he beat him, and left him all in Blood lying on the Ground, and crying out Murder. For this Fact the Scot was had before the Justice, who asking him, How he durst be so bold as to lay his profane Hands upon the Man of God? He, who knew very well what use to make of the Devil he had got, Foaming at the Mouth, and cunningly acting the Demoniack, made answer, That the Pape might thank himself for what he had met with; for since he had Conjured the Devil into him he spared no Body, neither Wife nor Children, nor would he spare the Justice himself, and with that fell a mangling and tearing the Magistrate, that he was fain to betake himself to his Heels, crying out, *O! the Devil, save me;*

and so the Scot marched home, no Man daring to lay hold on him, for fear of being torn to pieces by the Devil. But the Justice recollecting himself, sent for the Pape, told him; That the Scot was a cunning Rogue, and bid him go home, get a Plaister for his Head, and be silent, lest if the matter came to the Bishops Ears he might be Censured for going against the Rubrick of the Liturgy.

The Famous University where their Clergy are bred, is *Upsal*, 8 Swedish Miles from *Stockholme*. There are commonly 150, or 200 Students there, but no Endowed Colleges, as in other Countries. The Library is so mean and contemptible, that the Libraries of many Grammar Schools, and of private Men in *England* or *Holland* are far better stored with Books than it is. Upon viewing of it, and that of the Kings Palace, I called to mind the saying of a French Man, upon the like occasion; That *Swedeland* came behind *France* and *England* in the knowledge of Men and Things at least 800 years; yet some Swedes have been so conceited of the Antiquity of their Country, as to brag, that Paradice was seated in *Sweden*; that the Country was turned into such heaps of Rocks for the Rebellion of our first Parents, and that *Adam* and *Eve* had *Cain* and *Abel* in a Country three Swedish Miles distant from *Upsall*. A French Man standing by, and hearing this Romantick Story, as I was told, fitted him with

with the like, telling him, that when the World was made in six days, at the end of the Creation all the Rubbish that remained was thrown together into a Corner, which made up *Sweden* and *Norway*. And indeed, the French seem to have no great liking to the Country, whatever kindness they may have for the People; for a French Ambassador, as an Author of that Country relates, being by order of Queen *Christina*, Treated in a Country House four Swedish Miles from *Stockholme*, and upon the rode going and coming, with all the Varieties and Pleasures that the Country could afford, on purpose to make him have a good Opinion of the same; made answer to the Queen, (who asked him upon his return, What he thought of *Sweden*) That were he Master of the whole Country, he would presently Sell it, and Buy a Farm in *France* or *England*; which, under Favour, I think was a little Tart and Sawcy.

Having stayed a considerable time in *Swedeland*, and most part at *Stockholme*, I set out from thence to go to *Elsenbourg* by Land, and went a little out of my way to see a small City called *Eubrone*, Famous for a Coat of Arms which it got in this manner. A certain Masculine Queen of *Denmark*, who had Conquered a great part of *Sweden*, coming to this City, asked the Magistrates, What was the Arms of their City? Who having her, that they had none, she plucked up her Coats, and squatting upon the Snow, bid them take the mark she left there for their Arms; its pity she did not give them a suitable Motto to it also: What that Figure is called in Blazonery I know not, but to this Day the City uses it in their Arms, and for marking their Commodities. This Queen came purposely into *Sweden*, to pay a visit to a brave Woman, that opposed a King of *Swedeland*, who in a time of Famine would have put to Death all the Men and Women in his Country above 60 years of Age. The Country all the way I travelled in *Swedeland* is much of the same quality of the Land about *Stockholme*, until I came near the Province of *Schonen*, which is called the Storehouse, and Kitchin of *Sweden*, where the Country is far better. It was formerly very dangerous to Travel in this Province of *Schonen*, because of the Snaphances, who were a kind of Bloody Robbers, now utterly destroyed by the King; so that it is safe enough Travelling there. Entering into *Schonen* I saw 29 of these Rogues upon Wheels, and elsewhere in the Country, ten and twenty at several places. The King used great severity in destroying of them; some he caused to be broken upon the Wheel, others Spitted in at the Fundament, and out at the Shoulders, many had the Flesh pinched off of their Breasts, and so were fastened to

Stakes

Stakes till they Died; and others again had their Noses and both Hands cut off, and being seared with a hot Iron, were let go to acquaint their Comrades how they had been served. The King is very severe against Highway-Men and Duellers. In above a 100 Miles Travelling, we found not a House where there was either French Wine or Brandy, which made me tell a Swede of our Company, who was Travelling to *Denmark*, that I would undertake to shew any Man 500 Houses, wherein a Traveller might have Wine, and other good Accommodation in the space of an Hundred Miles upon any rode from *London*. There are several small Towns and fertile Land in this Country of *Sconen*, lying upon the *Sound*; at the narrowest part whereof lies *Elsenburg* burnt down by the *Danes* in the last War: Here I crost over to *Elsinore*, the passage being but a League broad.

The King of *Denmark* has a Castle at *Elsenore*, which commands the narrow passage of the *Sounds*, where all Ships that enter into, or come out of the *Baltick* Sea must pay Toll. Having visited this Castle, and staid about a Fortnight with the *English* Consul, and Sir *John Paul*, late Resident at the Court of *Swedeland*, I went to the *Danish* Court at *Copenhagen*.

Copenhagen is the Capital City of *Zeeland*, *Jutland*, or *Denmark*, and place of Residence of the King: It stands on a

K 3

Flat,

Flat, encompassed with a pleasant and delightful Country, much resembling *England*. The Streets of the City are kept very neat and clean, with Lights in the Night time for the convenience and safety of those who are then abroad; a Custom not as yet introduced into *Stockholme*, where it is dangerous to be abroad when it is dark. The Kings Men of War lie hear very conveniently, being orderly ranged betwixt Booms, after the manner of *Amsterdam*, and near the Admiralty House, which is a large pile of Building, well furnished with Stores and Magazins, secured by a Cittadel, that not only commands the City, but also the Haven, and entry into it. The Court of *Denmark* is splendid, and makes a far greater figure in the World than that of *Sweden*, though not many years ago, in the time of *Carolus Gustavus* the Father of the present King of *Swedeland*, it was almost reduced to its last, when the Walls of *Copenhagen* saved that Crown and Kingdom. That Siege was Famous, carried on with great vigour by the Swede, and as bravely maintained by the Danes: The Monuments whereof are to be seen in the Cannon Bullets gilt that still remain in the Walls of some Houses, and in the Steeple of the great Church of the Town. The Royal Palace in *Copenhagen* is but small, and a very ancient Building; but his Majesties House *Fredenburg* is a stately Fabrick of Modern Architecture, and

very

COPENHAGEN.

very richly Furnished. *Denmark* is at present a flourishing Kingdom, and the King, who hath now made it Hereditary, surpasses most of his Predecessors in Power and Wealth: He hath much enlarged his Dominions, as well as Authority; and by his Personal and Royal Virtues, no less than the eminent qualities of a great many able Ministers of State, he hath gained the Universal Love of his Subjects, and the esteem of all Foreign Princes and States. The Court is much frequented every day, but especially on Sundays, where about Eleven of the Clock in the Morning, the Nobility, Foreign Ministers, and Officers of the Army assemble, and make a glorious Appearance. There one may see many Knights of the Order of the Elephant of *Malto*; but I never saw any Order of the like Nature as that of *Sweden*, that King rarely appearing in his George and Garter; but on days of publick Audience I have observed at one time above 150 Coaches attending at the Court of *Denmark*, which are ten times more than ever I saw together at that of *Sweden*. The King is affable, and of easie access to Strangers, seen often abroad by his Subjects in his Gardens and Stables, which are very large, and well furnished with all sorts of Horses. He is a great lover of English Horses and Dogs, and delights much in Hunting, as his Eldest Son the Prince, with his Brothers do in Cock-fighting; insomuch

much, that the English Merchants cannot make a more acceptable present to those Princes, than of English Game-Cocks. The standing Forces of *Denmark* are well disciplined Men, and Commanded by good Officers, both Natives and Strangers, both French and Scots, as Major General *Duncan*, and Major General *Veldun*, both Scottish-Men, whom I saw at *Copenhagen*. The Soldiers as well as Courtiers are quartered upon the Citizens, a Custom which is likewise practised in *Sweden*, and tho' somewhat uneasie, yet not repined at by the People, who by the care and good Government of the King, find Trade much advanced. For his Majesty by encouraging Strangers of all Religions to live in his Dominions, and allowing the French and Dutch Calvinists, to have publick Churches, hath brought many Trading Families to *Copenhagen*, and by the measure he hath taken for setling Trade in prohibiting the Importation of Foreign Manufactures, and Reforming and new Modelling the East and West *India* Companies, hath much encreased Commerce, and thereby the Wealth of his Subjects; so that notwithstanding the new Taxes imposed upon all Coaches, Wagons, Ploughs, and all real and personal Estates, which amount to considerable Sums of Money; the People live very well and contented. There are commonly about 8000 Men in Garison in *Copenhagen*, and

his

his Majesties Regiment of Foot Guards, who are all Cloathed in Red, with Cloaks to keep them warm in the Winter time, is a very handsome Body of Men; and with the Horse Guards, who are bravely mounted, and have their Granadeers and Hautboys, make a very fine shew. His Majesty hath caused several new Fortifications to be built upon the *Elb*, and other Rivers, and hath now in his Possession, that strong Castle called *Hilgueland*, at present commanded by a Scottish-man. The Queen of *Denmark* is a most virtuous Princess, Sister to the present Landtgrave of *Hesse Cassel*, and in Perswasion a Calvinist, having a Chapel allowed her within the Court, though the publick Religion of the King and Kingdom be Lutheran. The Clergy here are Learned, many of them having studied at *Oxford* and *Cambridge*, where they learnt the English Language; and amongst the Bishops there is one Doctor *King* the Son of a Scottish-man. But seeing it is my design rather to observe the condition of the People, than to be punctual in describing all the Rarities that are remarkable in the Countries I have been in, I shall conclude what I have to say of *Denmark*, by acquainted the Reader, that the People of that Country live far better than the Swedes, and as well as most of their adjoyning Neighbours; and that there are several places, both there, and in *Norway*, which have the Names of English Towns, as *Arundale, Totness, London*, &c. When

When I first began to write this Treatise, I had some thoughts of making Observations upon the several Governments of other States and Dominions, where I had travelled some years before I was in the Countries I have been speaking of, as of the rest of *Germany, Hungary, Switzerlaud, Italy,* and *France*; but that was a Subject so large, and the usefulness of it to my present Design so inconsiderable, that by doing so, I found I could neither satisfie the Curious, by adding any thing material to those many who have already obliged the Publick by the Remarks of their Travels in those Places; or make my discontented Countrymen more averse than they are already from removing into those Countries, where I think few of them will chuse to transport themselves for the sake of Liberty and Property, though *England* were even worse than they themselves fancy it can be. All that remains to be done then, is to conclude this Treatise with an obvious and popular Remark, that those Countries, where Cities are greatest and most frequented by voluntary Inhabitants, are always the best to live in; and by comparing the City of *London* with all other Cities of *Europe*, and demonstrating by the Surveys I have made, (which I think will hardly be contradicted or confuted) that of all the Capital Cities of *Europe* it is the biggest and most populous, and to prove consequentially that *England*, for the generality of People, is the best Country in the World, especially for its Natives, to live in. Now this being an Observation (for what I know) not hitherto made good by Induction and Instance, (as I intend to do it) I hope it will please the Reader as much, as if I gave him a particular account of other Countries and Governments, and leave it to his own Reflection to state the Comparison.

Though *London* within the Walls cannot vye for bigness with many Cities of *Europe*; yet take the City and Suburbs together, according as it hath been survey'd by Mr. *Morgan*, in breadth from St. *George*'s Church in *Southwark* to *Shoreditch*, and in length from *Limehouse* to *Petty-France* in *Westminster*, and it is in a vast proportion larger in compass of Ground, and number of Houses, than any City in *Europe* whatsoever. This I shall demonstrate first, by comparing it with some Cities of *Holland*, and then with the most considerable Cities of the other Countries of *Europe*, which I shall set down in an Alphabetical Order, with the number of the Houses they severally contain.

When *London* and Suburbs was surveyed some years ago by Mr. *Morgan*, there were reckoned to be in it 84000 Houses, besides Hospitals, Alms-houses, and other Buildings, that paid no Chimney-money to the King:
Now

Now if those were added, and the vast number of new Houses that have been built since that Survey, upon modest computation *London* may be reckoned to contain 100000 Houses; nay, 'tis believed 120000, which truly considering the extraordinary Additions that have been made lately, is not improbable; I know the *French* vapour, and would perswade the World, that *Paris* is much bigger than *London*. And the *Hollanders* will scarce believe, that *London* hath more Houses than the 18 Cities in *Holland* that have Voices in the States, for (say they) *Amsterdam* stands upon 1000 Morgans of Land, and *London* stands but upon 1800. To both which I answer, That it is very true that *Paris* takes up a great spot of Ground, but then you must consider, that in *Paris* there are several hundreds of Monasteries, Churches, Colleges, and Cloisters, some of them having large Gardens, and that in *Paris* there are 7500 Palaces and Ports for Coaches, which have likewise great Gardens; whereas *London* is very thick built, and in the City the Houses have scarce a Yard big enough to set a Pump or House of Conveniency in; but the Weekly Bills of Mortality will decide this Question, and plainly give it to *London*, and so doth Monsieur *la Cour*, and Sir *William Petty* in his last Essays dedicated to the King, making it appear, that *London* is bigger than *Paris*, *Roan*,

and

and *Rochel* altogether; and as for *Amsterdam*, I do appeal to all knowing Men that have seen it, that although it be true, that it stands upon 1000 Morgans of Land, yet there is not above 400 Morgans built; and this I prove thus, that the large Gardens, on the *Heeregraft*, *Kysersgraft*, and *Princegraft*, and the Burghwalls of *Amsterdam*, take up more than a third part of the City; then reckon the Bastions, and the space of Ground between the Wall and the Houses, and all the Ground unbuilt from the *Utricks-Port*, to the *Wesoper-Port*, *Muyer-Port*, and so to the Seaside, and you will find it to be near 300 *Morgens* of Land: There are two Parishes in the Suburbs of *London*, viz. *Stepney*, and *St. Martins in the Fields*, (the latter being so big, that the Parliament divided it into four Parishes) either of them have more Houses than *Rotterdam* or *Haerlem*; and there are several other great Parishes, as *St. Margarets Westminster*, *St. Giles in the Fields*, *St. Olaves*, and *St. Mary Saviours*, the which if they stood apart in the Country would make great Cities; we reckon in *London*, and the Suburbs thereof to be at least 130 Parishes, which contains 100000 Houses; now if you reckon 8 Persons to every House, then there are near 800000 Souls in *London*, but there are some that say, there is a Million of Souls in it: I shall now set down the Cities Alphabetically, and their number of Houses, as they were given to me

A Description of

me not only from the Surveyors and City Carpenters, but from the Books of the Hearth-Money, and Collectors of the several Taxes in the respective Cities: And first I shall begin with the 18 Cities that have Voices in the States of *Holland*.

Cities in HOLLAND.

Cities.	Houses.
1. Dort	5500
2. Haerlem	7250
3. Delft	2300
4. Leyden	13800
5. Amsterdam	25460
6. Rotterdam	8400
7. Gouda	3540
8. Gorcom	2460
9. Schiedam	1550
10. Briell	1250
11. Schonehoven	2200
12. Alckmaar	1540
13. Horn	3400
14. Enckhuysen	5200
15. Edam	2000
16. Monekendam	1500
17. Medenblick	850
18. Purmerent	709

Total 88909

Cities

CITIES and HOUSES.

Cities in GERMANY, and in the Seventeen Provinces.

Cities.	Houses.
1. Antwerp	1850
2. Aix la Chapelle	2250
3. Arford	8440
4. Berlin	5200
5. Bon	410
6. Brisack	1200
7. Breme	9200
8. Breda	3420
9. Bolduke	6240
10. Bergen op Zome	2120
11. Brussels	19200
12. Cologne	12000
13. Cleave	640
14. Coblentz	420
15. Castels	1520
16. Dresden	6420
17. Disseldorpe	620
18. Dunkirk	2440
19. Emden	2400
20. Francfort	10200
21. Groningen	8400
22. Guant	18200
23. Harford	1420
24. Hanouer	1850
25. Heidelberg	7520
26. Hambourg	12500
27. Lubeck	6500
28. Louain	8420

29. Lypsick

144 CITIES and HOUSES.

29.	Lypsick	3242
30.	Lunenburg	3100
31.	Lewardin	5860
32.	Mayence	2420
33.	Malin	8000
34.	Middelburg	6200
35.	Madelburg	1120
36.	Mastricht	5600
37.	Munster	1240
38.	Nurenburg	18240
39.	Osenburg	2200
40.	Osburg	8420
41.	Oldenburg	620
42.	Praag	18640
43.	Passaw	560
44.	Ratisbonne	6540
45.	Strasbourg	8560
46.	Spire	540
47.	Stockholm	6480
48.	Salsburg	12460
49.	Uytrick	8240
50.	Vienna	4520
51.	Vean	340
52.	Wormes	1200
53.	Westburg	2420

Total 314460

Cities

CITIES and HOUSES.

Cities in FRANCE.

Cities.	Houses.
1. Avignion	12400
2. Amiens	5200
3. Bullion	1400
4. Bomont	800
5. Burdeaux	8420
6. Callis	1324
7. Caine	2147
8. Chalons	1850
9. Diepe	1920
10. Lyons	16840
11. Montrevil	820
12. Montpeiller	5240
13. Marselles	9100
14. Nantes	4420
15. Nismes	3120
16. Orleans	10200
17. Orange	354
18. Paris	72400
19. Rochel	4200
20. Roan	11200
21. Tolouze	13200
22. Valence	458
Total	187013

Cities in ITALY.

Cities.		Houses.
1.	Bolonia	12400
2.	Florence	8520
3.	Genoua	17200
4.	Luca	1650
5.	Legorne	3560
6.	Milan	18500
7.	Naples	17840
8.	Pisa	2290
9.	Padua	8550
10.	Rome	31200
11.	Sena	1820
12.	Venice	24870
13.	Veterba	620
14.	Valentia	1520
	Total	155040

Cities in SAVOY.

Cities.		Houses.
1.	Chambray	852
2.	Salé	320
3.	Turin	8540
4.	Nice	500
5.	St. John de Lateran	420
6.	Rennes	340
7.	Maly	270
	Total	11242

CITIES and HOUSES. 147

Cities in SWITZERLAND.

Cities.	Houses.
1. Berne	4270
2. Bale	5120
3. Geneva	4540
4. Losana	2100
5. Solure	500
6. Zurick	6200
7. Morge	210
8. Vina	320
9. St. Morrice	300
Total	23560

Cities in DENMARK.

Cities.	Houses.
1. Copenhagen	8220
2. Elsenore	
Total	

Cities in SWEEDLAND.

Cities.	Houses.
1. Northoanen	600
2. Stockholme	7500
3. Upsal	8200
Total	16300

AN EXACT RELATION OF THE ENTERTAINMENT

Of His Most Sacred Majesty

WILLIAM III.

KING of *England,*
Scotland, France and *Ireland*;

Hereditary Stadtholder of the *United Netherlands, &c.*

At the *HAGUE.*

Giving a particular Description of His MAJESTY's Entry there, *Jan.* 26. 169¾. And of the several Triumphant Arches, Pyramids, Pictures, *&c.* with the Inscriptions and Devices.

Illustrated with Copper Plates of the whole Solemnity, exactly drawn from the Original.

Translated from the Dutch.

LONDON:
Printed in the Year M. DC; XCI.

AN
Exact Relation

Of the ENTERTAINMENT of His Moſt Sacred Majeſty,

WILLIAM III.
At the *HAGUE.*

HIS Majeſty being earneſtly Entreated by the States of *Holland*, and the Confederate Princes in *Germany, &c.* to meet at a General Congreſs, to be held at the *Hague*, in order to Concert matters for the next Campaign, was pleaſed to Condeſcend to their Requeſt, and hazard His Royal Perſon by Sea, (though in the depth of Winter) His Noble Zeal for the Good of us in particular, and *Europe* in general, ſurmounting all thoſe Difficulties: Whereupon he accordingly took Shipping on the Sixteenth of *January* 169¾. in a Yacht, then lying at *Gravesend*, and set Sail that Afternoon, being attended by divers Yatchts and Men of War, and a Noble Retinue of Persons of the best Quality; but by Reason of the very thick Mists, and consequently little Wind, was four days before he could make the Coast of *Holland*; yet, at last, when he arrived within two or three Leagues of *Goree*, His Majesty ventured to go a Shoar in the Boat, attended by the Duke of *Ormond*, the Earl of *Portland*, and my Lord *Overkirke*, &c. and another Boat, but most unfortunately there fell so thick a Fog, and the Ice surrounded them so closely, that neither could they make the Shoar, nor get back to the Ship, but were forc'd to lie still for two and twenty Hours, enduring the most bitter Cold, and without (almost) hopes of ever getting alive on Shoar: All which, His Majesty bore with His wanted Magnanimity and Courage, and when one of the Boat-men too freely expressed his Fear of Death, he reproved him with this Noble saying, *What are you afraid to Die in my Company.* But it pleased the Almighty Providence, at length to dissipate the Mist, and Conduct His Royal Majesty safely to the Shoar, and on the 21st of *January*, about half an hour after Ten, landed at the *Orange Polder*, at the Mouth of the *Maese*, a little below *Maseland-Sluyce*, but by the long continuance

tinuance in the Cold, was so Benummed, that he could hardly either stand or Speak. From hence His Majesty went immediately to the House of the Heer Van *Rynenbergh*, where having refreshed Himself, and Dined, He hasted to *Houisflaerdyke*, where He was met, and Congratulated with all Demonstrations of Respects and Joy, by the Deputies of the States; as also by Prince *Casimir* of *Nassau*, Stadtholder of *Friezeland*, whom His Majesty received with all the Marks of the most tender Affection imaginable, Embracing and Kissing them with great Ardency. Prince *Nassau Sarbruggen*, the Count Van *Hoern*, and divers other Persons of Quality, here likewise Congratulated His Majesties happy arrival, who were all most kindly received by His Majesty.

'Twas expected that the King would have lain here this Night, and so have entred the *Hague* by day light; but on the contrary, His extraordinary Desire of entring immediately upon Business, would not let Him give Himself so much as one Nights ease; And His Majesty, after a very short Refreshment here, departed for the *Hague*, attended with five or six Coaches with six Horses: In His own Coach accompanied Him the Earl of *Portland*, and the Lord *Overkirk*, arriving at the *Hague* about half an hour after five in the Evening; where (though he was not that Night expected) there wanted not

the

the general Acclamations of the People of all sorts, who run by His Coach, crying out, *Long Live King* William, *Welcom, Welcom, &c.* His Majesty Rode through the Triumphant Arches, Erected by the Lords of the *Hague*, and the Honourable the Lords Committee of the Council of *Holland*, (of which we shall give an exact Description in their proper Places) directly to the Court, where being arrived, and the Gates shut to keep out the extraordinary press of People, thirty peices of Cannon, which were planted upon the *Vyverberg*, were thrice discharged, Publick Thanksgivings were made in all the Churches, and the Bells rung with great Joy; and throughout the Town almost all the Houses were Illuminated with great numbers of Candles in their Windows, whilst all the People, Rich and Poor, Old and Young, made all Demonstrations of their inexpressible Joy for His Majesties most happy Arrival.

That Evening the Earl of *Berka*, Envoy Extraordinary from the Emperor, waited upon His Majesty, and was a long time in private with Him; and the next day several Members of the States, and divers Persons of Quality came to Compliment His Majesty, and Congratulate His Arrival.

The Ministers of the several Confederate Princes, who upon the Kings arrival had sent Expresses to their respective Masters,

assembling

assembling themselves in Congress; immediately after their breaking up, the Imperial, Spanish, and Brandenburgh Envoys, came to wait upon His Majesty; as also the Council of State, and the Lords of the General Accounts, with all their Members, to Congratulate and Complement Him.

The King immediately applied Himself to the Affairs of State, and taking first into His Consideration the Sea Affairs, gave the Command of the Dutch Fleet to the Heer *Cornelius* Van *Tromp*, with the Title of Vice-Admiral of *Holland*, who gratefully accepted the same, and immediately beat up his Drums for Seamen, who flocked to him in great abundance. His Majesty gave also out Commissions for two Regiments of *Mariners* to be raised.

The Elector of *Brandenburgh*, who had waited some time at *Cleave*, as soon as he received advice of His Majesties arrival, set forward for the *Hague*.

In the mean time it was Desired, and Agreed to by His Majesty, That His Majesty would Please to Honour the *Hague* with a Publick Entry, on *Monday*, *January* the 26th: Whereupon the Trained Bands, and the Guards were ordered to be ready; And accordingly on *Monday*, at two of the Clock in the Afternoon, His Majesty went out of the Town by the way of the *Vyverberg*, to the North-end, and from thence

round

round the Wall to the West-end, and so to the *Hounslaerdyke*, or *Loosduyn*'s-bridge, where began the Triumph. Over this Bridge was Erected, by the Burghermasters of the *Hague*, a Triumphant Arch, the Figure whereof we have here Represented. Over the Arch in the Front, is a Man and a Woman standing at an Altar Sacrificing, with the Words, *Io Triumphe*. On the top of all stands the Statue of His Majesty, with a Staff in His right Hand, at the top of which is a Cypher of His Name, with a Crown. On the two Columns of the Arch, on one side are these Words,

Ob Cives Servatos: For having preserved his Country-men.
Ob Hostes Fugatos: For having destroyed his Enemies.

and on the other side,

Restitutis Provinciis: The Provinces being Restored.
Libertatis Regnis: The Kingdoms being Delivered.

Behind each Column is a small Oval, in one a Lawrel with this Word,

Victoria, Victory,

on the other a Palm, with the Word,

Clementia, Mercy.

Here His Majesty was received by the Magistrates of the *Hague*, who Complimented

ted Him, and Congratulated His Arrival, the Pensionary *Vander Hoeck* being their Speaker, who humbly Thanked the King in the Name of the Magistrates and Burghers, for the Honour His Majesty was pleased to do them by His Presence, in a most Eloquent Oration.

From hence was a Lane made on each side by the Burghers in Arms, who appeared in very great Splendour, being most of them very richly clad, many having been at great Expence for their Equipage.

These Trained Bands consist of six Companies, of about two and three Hundred Men in each Company; they make in all about Fifteen Hunderd Men: These standing in their Order, reached all along the West-end, the great Market, the High Street, and so to the Court-yard.

All along this way, quite up to the Court, before the Houses and Stalls, were built Scaffolds, which were filled by a vast multitude of Spectators, who scrupled not to give an 100 Guilders in some places for the use of a Chamber during the Shew. The number of Spectators being the greatest that has ever been seen in the *Hague*; insomuch, that one would have judged all the Inhabitants of *Holland* to have been in this Town.

After the Pensionary had ended his Speech, and His Majesty kindly Thanked them, the Cavalcade proceeded. First went two very rich

rich Coaches with six Horses, in which were divers Persons of Quality, next the Kings Life Guard, the Officers in extraordinary rich Equipage: After them a great number of Lacquees and Footmen all in the Kings Livery, and black Velvet Caps; after them came the Kings Pages, Gentlemen, and Servants on Horseback, in extraordinary rich Liveries. Then came His Majesty riding in a large, and very richly Gilt Coach, drawn by Six White Stone Horses, accompanied by the Lord *Overkirk* on the left Hand, and the Earls of *Monmouth* and *Scarborough* over-against him. On each side of the Coach the Switzers with their Halbards, in rich Livery Coats also, walked on Foot. The Provost General *Urck*, and the Heer *Roulas* Captain of the Switzers rid on Horseback immediately before the Kings Coach, and after it came about Twelve Coaches with Six Horses, wherein Rid the Duke of *Norfolk*, the Earls of *Devonshire* and *Portland*, the Bishop of *London*, and several other English Noblemen; as also the chief Ministers of the Government, and the Magistrates of the *Hague*, besides these, were many Coaches with Four Horses.

The King as he passed along, was Saluted, and Complimented by divers Persons of Quality, which His Majesty returned with great Kindness, often looking out of the Coach, with great Satisfaction upon the People,

Entertainment at the Hague.

People, who shouted with extraordinary Chearfulness, crying out, *Long Live the King our Stadtholder*, &c.

The Stadthouse, by which the King was to Ride, was Beautified with Seven very Noble Transparent Pictures; behind which they put Lights in the Evening, which were set off with Garlands of made Flowers: Above in the middle, was the King and Queen, and on each side of them another Picture; One of a Lion with this Motto,

Placidum venerantur, & horrent infestum: They Worship him when he is Calm, and Dread him when he is Angry;

the other of an Unicorn, with this Motto,

Nihil passa Veneni: She can endure no Poison.

Underneath there are three other Pictures, one of a Crane sitting upon his Nest, clapping his Wings upon break of a Day, and Sun Rising, with this Motto,

Recreatur ab Ortu: He is refreshed by the Rising.

the other of an Atlas bearing the World upon his bending Shoulders, resting with his Breast upon a small Hill, with this Motto,

In te Domus inclinata recumbit: The leaning House rests on Thee.

The Third, a Crane standing on his Nest, and chattering upon the Rising of the Sun, with this Motto,

Vidit & Exaltavit: He saw it and was glad.

In the Court of Justice by the side of the Stadthouse, a Pillar was Erected four Rows high, garnished with Coats of Arms; upon which towards Night they set great numbers of Flambeaux.

The Lords of the *Hague* raised also a Rich and a Glorious Triumphal Arch in Honour of this great Monarch, in the Market Place: This was done upon the Account of his having been Born there; which as they look upon to be one of the greatest Glories of the Place, and whereof hereafter they will have the greatest Reason to Boast, so they were desirous to shew what Sence they had of it, upon so very Glorious an occasion.

This is much the highest Arch of them all; without any Pillars, and on both sides are many Pictures done in light Colour; and just over the passage there are two others done upon Silk, and Transparent, so as that by Lights, which were set behind them in the Evening, they appeared very Gloriously.

At the top of all was placed a Sphear, and above that, *Fame* Sounding a Trumpet in a flying posture, and leading a *Pegasus*; with Trophies at each Corner.

Behind this Arch, towards the High-street, the Arms of the Emperor *Adolphus*, (who was Descended of the House of *Nassau*) were set up; and over them the Sixteen Quarters of His Majesties Arms: But those that managed

naged this matter, not understanding it so well as they ought to have done, they have committed several Mistakes, which in the Graving I have altered: It is to no purpose to set down the particulars, which lie chiefly in the stating of the several Scutcheons, according to the precedency of the Kingdoms over which His Majesties Ancestors had the Governments, which though they are not generally taken notice of by ordinary Observers; yet, since upon such Solemnities, the curiousest and most inquisitive Men are always present, it was much to be Wished, that those Things had been more exactly regulated.

There were several Inscriptions round the Arch: On the Front above the Gate, and under the Arms of the *Hague*, was this,

Hic Incunabula Divum: Here was the Cradle of the Gods.

[*Incunabula* are properly the Swadling-Cloths in which new Born Infants are wrapt up.]

Above, beneath, and on both sides was Writ,

Nobilium primo, Ducum Maximo, Posthumo Gulielmo III. Cælitus dat. To the chiefest of Noblemen, the greatest of Dukes, [or Generals, the word being ambiguous, coming after Noblemen] the *Posthumous William III. given from Heaven.*

And behind above the Pictures,

Victoriis, Trophæis, Fortissimo Imperatori, Destinate, Cautissimo Gubernatori, and underneath at the bottom of the Arch,

Quatuor Regnorum Regi, Fœderati Belgii Gubernatori, Gulielmo III. Virtute & Triumphis fulgenti, Grati Animi & Letitiæ publicæ Signum hoc erexit Haga Comitis.

i. e. The Hague *Erected this as a Testimony of her Gratitude, and of the publick Joy for the Victories and Trophies of* William III. *King of Four Kingdoms, Stadtholder of the United Provinces, equally Glorious for his Virtue and his Success.*

On each side of the Arch there are two Wings, which make a Semi-Circle; within each of which are Seven Pictures representing the Battels and Victories of the former Princes of *Orange* by Sea and Land; every Picture having an Inscription under it.

On the First, on the Right Hand, *Patientia læsa fit furor: Injured Patience turns to Rage:* Intimating, that they had endured the Insolencies of the Spaniards as long as was possible, and that at last they were forced to Rise.

On the Second, *Res poscit Opem, & Conspirat Amice: The Matter needs help, and Prospers by Friendly Conference.*

On the Third, *Per Tela, per Undas: Through Weapons and Waves.*

On the Fourth, *Audentes Deus ipse juvat: God himself helps the daring.*

On the Fifth, *Tantas dedit Unio vires: Such Strength has Union given.*

Entertainment at the Hague.

On the Sixth, *Aquilas & Mænia cepit*: *He took Standards and Cities.*

On the Seventh, *Celsas superat virtute Carinas*: *He Conquers tall Ships by his Valour.*

On the first Picture of the left Hand, *Repetenda quiescunt Arma virum*: *The Arms of the brave are at rest, hereafter to be resumed again.*

On the Second, *Non uno Virtus contenta Triumpho*: *Virtue not content with one Triumph.*

On the Third, *Crescunt numero crescente Trophæa*: *As the number encreases so do their Trophies too.*

On the Fourth, *Cæsorum replebant Funera Campos*: *The Funerals of the Slain filled all the Fields.*

On the Fifth, *Ultra Garamantas & Indos*: *Beyond the furthermost parts of the Earth.*

On the Sixth, *Fortis Promissa Juventæ*: *The promisses of valiant Youth.*

On the Seventh, *Deos in prælia confert*: *He brings the Gods to Combat for him.*

Between these Wings there are two Pyramids fixt upon Pedestals, each having a Picture in the Front: In that on the Right side, there is a Circle made up of Hearts, with this Inscription, *Hanc accipe Magne Coronam*: *Great Hero accept this Crown.*

In that on the Left side, there is an Altar with Incense, and this Inscription, *Thure tuo redolent Aræ*: *The Altars yeild a fragrant Smell with thy Frankincense.*

These Pyramids have each of them before them three Transparent Pictures, containing Hieroglyphicks and Trophies of Victory; The Pyramids being covered on the sides with Green: On one of these Pyramids was set the Kings Picture; on the other the Queens, at full length: On that of the Kings was this Inscription, *Quis gratior appulit Oris*: What more acceptable Person ever touched our Coasts. Upon the Queens, *Reprimit & Refigit*: She Represses and Re-establishes.

Over the Wings, the Figures of the Four late Princes of *Orange* are set up; and under each some marks of Victory. Under *William* the First, *Patriæ Liberatori*: To the Deliverer of his Country. Under Prince *Maurice*, *Gloriæ Vindici*: The Vindicator of our Glory. Under *Frederick-Henry*, *Libertatis Assertori*: The Assertor of our Liberty. And under Prince *William* the Second, *Publicæ Felicitatis Statori*: To the Establisher of the publick Happiness.

The Triumphal Arch in the Court.

PAssing from hence to the High-street they met another Triumphal Arch, which represents a pleasant Building, Beautified on both sides with Pillars of red and white Marble, the Body of the Work being of black and white Marble; the Bases and Chapiters are gilt: It has two large Pictures before, and

and as many behind, Painted in lively Colours; those before, representing a Roman Field Battle and Sea Fight; those behind, one War, the other Peace: That of War has the World in a Flame, with several Figures, some Dead; others Living, make Justice lie down in Distress: That of Peace has a Globe, upon which stand Justice and Peace embracing one another, whilst *Pan* and his Companions make themselves Merry with the Fruits of the Earth. Over all in the middle of the Arch, on a Pedestal, stands the Statue of the King on Horseback, as big as the Life, and painted like Brass; on both sides of the Pedestal there is this Inscription, *Regi Triumphanti: To the Triumphing King*. Over his Head, which is adorned with Green, there are two Wreaths placed cross ways, and over them a Royal Crown and Scepter, and underneath a Cross.

On both sides of the Arch there are two Squares, wherein are set, both behind and before, transparent Pictures for the convenience of setting Lights behind in the Evening. On the outside of these Squares there was Painted a Cloudy Pillar, and a Pillar of Fire, with the Corners adorned with Green.

On the gilded Frize of the Arch there is this Inscription, *Soloque, Saloque, in reprimenda Tyrannide, & Restituenda Seculi Felicitate*: By Land and by Sea, for repressing Tyranny,

ranny, and Restoring the Happiness of the Age. And on the sides of the aforesaid Frizes are these Words, *Heroibus Priori: To him who is above Heroes. Antiquis Majori: Greater than the Antients.*

On the sides of the Pedestal, on which stands the Kings Horse, there are two Suits of Armour gilt, and two cover'd with Silver, with a Plume of Feathers over them; besides other Marks of Triumph, as Shields, Standards, *&c.* Before is the King of *England*'s Arms, and behind his Cypher.

At each end of the Arch there are two Wings, upon which on both sides there were several Histories Painted on white and black; as of *Hercules, Theseus, Phaëthon, Perseus* and *Andromeda,* with the Arms of *England, Scotland, France* and *Ireland.* Under all, quite round the Arch, there are these Words, *Sceptris, Exercitibus, Classibus, Votis, Augusto, Armato, Parato, Recepto*; which ought to be Read thus, *Augusto Sceptris, Armato Exercitibus, Parato Classibus, Recepto Votis: August by his Crowns, Defended by his Armies, Ready with his Fleet, Received with Acclamations.*

Within the Arch of either side, there are two Pictures; one of *Europe,* to show its Glory, with a Bull on one side, and this Motto, *Eripe Raptori Miseram: Deliver the Miserable from her Ravisher.* The other, *Neptune,* carrying *Thetis* over the Sea, with this Motto, *Mea jura Tuere: Defend my Rights.*

Over

Over the Passage, is this Inscription, *Haga posuit Consulum Decreto*: The Hague Erected it by the Burghermasters Order.

The Triumphal Arch in the outward Court, at the Entrance of the Court Gate.

THis Triumphal Arch was Erected by the Order of their High and Mighty Lordships, the Committee of the Council of *Holland*: It is of the Dorick Order, after the Italian manner, with three Passages, and the middle higher than the rest of the Building. It stands upon Eight Pillars of each side, supported by broad Pedestals, each whereof bears two Pillars: Over the middle Passage there is a Cupola of an Octogenal Figure, whereon upon a Pedestal stands the Statue of His Majesty on Horseback, as big as the Life, all richly gilt; two Prisoners lie by the Pedestal Chained with their Backs to it, done over with Copper: The whole Arch is Painted of a Free-Stone Colour; the whole intercolumniation of both sides, is beautified with Pictures drawn in white and black, with Histories of the Heroick and Illustrious Actions of this great Monarch. Over these Eight Pillars are placed Eight Figures of both Sexes, as big as the Life, of a Copper Colour. On that side which faces the Viver, is the Representation of a Victory at Sea, and a *Neptune* lying down with his Trident, with this Inscription, *Triumphet in Undis*: *Let him Triumph in the Waves.* Towards the Lane, Trophies of Victory by Land, with this Motto, *Attingat Solium Jovis*: *Let him reach to* Jupiter's *Throne.*

These Words are Written round the Cupola of this Building, *Pio, Felici, Inclyto, Triumphanti, Patriæ Patri Gulielmo III. Gubernatori P. C. J. P. Restauratori Belgii Fœderati, Liberatori Angliæ, Servatori Scotiæ, Pacificatori Hiberniæ, Reduci*: To the *Pious*, Happy, Renowned William III. *Triumphant, Father of his Country*, *Stadtholder and Restorer of the* United Netherlands, *Redeemer of* England, *Preserver of* Scotland, *Quieter of* Ireland, *now return'd home.*

On the Front, under the Images, towards the outer Court, there are Four Spaces, upon which are these Inscriptions.

In the First, *Post Maximas res Domi forisque Gestas, Arctissimo cum Principibus icto Fœdere, Suorum Vindex, Defensor Oppressorum*: *After having done Glorious Things, at home and abroad, having made a most firm Alliance with other Princes, He is become the Avenger of His own Peoples Wrongs, and a Defender of the Oppressed.* Under this there is a Pannel, on which is a great Picture, in which several brave Men are described Fighting against a Dragon, with this Motto, *Uniti Fortius obstant*: *They make the firmer Resistance being United.*

In

In the Second Space, *Mare Transvectus liberat Britanniam, & late Dominantibus Ornatus Sceptris, in Patriam publicâ cum Lætitiâ receptus est*: Crossing the Seas He delivered Britain, where being Honoured with Scepters of large extended Power, He is received again into his own Country with publick Joy. Underneath in the small Pannel, there is a Ballance, and in one Scale several Crowns, in the other a Sword, which outweighs the Crowns, with this Motto, *Præmia non Æquant*: The Rewards do not equal the Merit.

In the Third Space, *Lugente Patriâ, Mærente Europâ, Afflictâ Antiquissimâ Nassaviorum Stirpe, Heroum, Imperatorum, Principum Fæcundâ*: His Country Mourning, Europe Grieving, the most autient Family of Nassau, which was fruitful of Heroes, Emperors and Princes, Lamenting. And in the Pannel, there is described a burning Phœnix, with a young one arising out of her Ashes, and this Motto, *Prælucet Posthuma Proles*: His Posthumous Issue shines the brighter. This is designed for *William* the Second, who died without Issue, leaving the Princess Royal with Child of His Majesty.

In the Fourth Space, *Gulielmum, Posthumum, Britannorum, Arausionensium Tertium, Patriæ Spem, Reipublicæ Palladium*: William the Posthumous, the Third of Britain and Orange, His Countries Hope, the Palladium of the Commonwealth. His Birth is described upon the Picture,

&cture, and three Crowns with a Scepter upon the Pannel, with this Motto, *Tenues ornant Diademate Cunæ: His tender Cradle adorns the Diadem.*

On that side towards the inner Court, there are on the Fronts four other Spaces.

In the First Space, there is this Inscription, *Fatum Europæ favens de Cælo dedit, futuram portendens, Majestatem, admodum Puerum, exemplar constituit. A favourable Fate to Europe gave him from Heaven, and portending future Majesty, set Him for a pattern when he was yet very Young.* Underneath His Education is described, with a young Eagle Soaring against the Sun Beams upon the Pannel, with this Motto, *Tener adversis enititur alis: Though Young he bears up against it with His Wings.*

In the Second Space, *Qui Juventute Strenuè Transactâ, Funestis jactatâ bellis ac dissidiis in tanto rerum discrimine: Who spent his Youth bravely, whilst it was tossed about by Bloody Wars and Discords, the publick being in such dangerous Circumstances.* Upon the Pannel there is a Castle standing upon a Hill, with a Pike by it, and two Lawrels springing out of it, with this Motto, *Contorta Triumphos portendit: When wreathed together it portends Triumphs.*

In the Third Space, *Nutantis Belgii, quà Mari, quà Terrà, admotus in Pristinum Decus Gubernaculi, Gloriam, Aras & Focos asseruit:*

He being Restored to His Antient Dignity and Government, Defended the Religion and Properties of the tottering Low Countries both by Sea Land: On the Pannel there is a Ship row'd by Men in Armour, with this Motto, *Alter erit Typhis: There shall be another Typhis.*

In the Fourth Space, *Meritis Famam Superantibus Trophæis, Principi Atavis Regibus Editæ Felicibus junctus Hymenæis: His deserved Trophies out doing even Fame, He was happily joyned in Wedlock to a Princess descended from an Antient Race of Kings.* The Picture represents Their Majesties Marriage; and there are also in the Pannel an Unicorn and a Lyon moving together; and the Unicorn Goaring of Serpents and Vipers, with this Motto, *Virusque Fugant, Viresque Repellunt: They both drive away the Poison, and repel the Strength.*

At the top, upon the Pedestal of the Kings Statue before, there are these Words, *Populi Salus: The Peoples Happiness.* And behind, *Procerum Decus: The Honour of the Nobility.*

Upon the great Cupola there are four distinct Histories Painted in four Pannels.

The First has this Motto, *Refert Saturnia Regna: He brings back the Saturnian Reign.*

The Second this, *Novos Orbes, nova Sceptra paramus: We prepare new Worlds, and new Scepters.*

The Third this, *Superare & parcere vestrum est: It is your part to Conquer and to Spare.*

The

The Fourth this, *Cætera Transibunt*: Other Things shall pass away.

Over the small Arch on both sides, the Arms of *England* were placed, with their Supporters: Over the great Arch the Arms of *Holland* were placed, with two flying Images of Fame blowing of Trumpets.

A Description of the Fireworks, with their Representations.

IN the Canal behind the Court, upon a large Scaffold, there were very fine Fireworks prepared, which were Lighted the Evening after His Majesty entred the *Hague*.

In the middle was the Kings Cypher, with a Crown over it: On the sides stood two high Pyramids, a Lyon, a *Hercules*, and a Sun: On each Corner of the Scaffold there were four Cases of Rockets, four of which were much larger then the rest, which represented the four Kingdoms of *England*, *Scotland*, *France* and *Ireland*, with the Arms of those Kingdoms: Round about there was

Enterainment at the Hague.

Pallissado stuck with Rockets, some Orange colour, some white, some blew, placed alternately to the number of Three Hunderd and Fifty.

They placed Fifteen Bulwarks round the Scaffold, on which they had mounted Cannon and Mortar pieces: Between which they had large Mortars made like Beehives and Pumps, which were charged with several sorts of Fireworks.

About half an hour after Six in the Evenning, the Fireworks were Lighted: Just before Thirty pieces of Cannon that were planted upon the Wall of the Viver were discharged; then follow'd Twenty five Mortar shot on both sides of the Scaffold, and afterwards the Crown and Cypher, *WR.* which appeared like 350 Pearls shining in the Air.

About the Pallissadoes they had planted several Devices: Towards the States Chamber was one with these Words, *Triumphat semper Augustus: He Triumphs always August.* On each side of this there was one planted; One was, *Offensum metuunt Hostes: His Enemies Dread him when he is Offended.* The other, *Carum venerantur Amici: His Friends Worship Him who is so dear to them.* These shining very bright in the Air, made a very pleasant show.

Over the Cipher and Crown was a Ship toss'd about as in a Storm, with this Motto,

Ne metuas, Cæsarem vehis: Fear not, thou carriest Cæsar. This also was visible in the Air.

When the Pyramids were Fired, they gave a lowd buzzing Noise, which was now and then Answered by the Mortars.

Then the Belgick Lyon, and the *Hercules*, play'd very wonderfully. *Hercules*'s Arms were Expanded, firing with Eight several Pauses, to denote his Labours, which were. 1. *The Establishment of Religion and Liberty.* 2. *The securing the Tranquillity of* Europe. 3. *The Settlement of the Government upon a right Bottom.* 4. *The Preservation of the Common Interests of the People.* 5. *The Preservation of Unity amongst the Neighbouring Princes.* 6. *The clearing of the Sea, and the increasing of Trade.* 7. *The Advancement of the Glory of this State.* 8. *The concluding of a firm and lasting Peace.*

While the Fire play'd so finely, the Air was full of the crackling Noise, and the Buzzes of the several sorts of Fireworks, and they continued so very thick, that it did in a good measure dispel the Fog, which was then very thick. At times they lighted Water-Balls, Water-Candles, Water-Bullets, Water-Boats, Water-Morters, Rats and Dolphins in a Vessel upon the Canal, which sputtering and crackling upon the Water, gave an Entertainment so great, that several Ingenious Men, who understood these Matters, owned, that they had never seen any Thing like it. They

Entertainment at the Hague. 25

They kindled also some Hundreds of pitch Barrels set round the Scaffold, which encreased the light, whereby the other Works which play'd all the while, were discerned the better. It lasted till about Eight, and was ended with Twenty five Mortar-shot; after which the Cannon were several times discharged: The whole was done without any Mischance, save only the loss of one Gunner, who sweeping a Cannon, lost both his Hands, and died of his Wounds. When His Majesty came to Court, the Militia stood in order in the outer Court, before the Triumphal Arch, *viz.* Baron *Friesem*'s Regiment of Foot, Baron *Heyde*'s Regiment of Horse, who having discharged all together, went to the *Viverbergh* to give way to the Train Bands in Arms. Several of the Lords of the States were in the Council Chamber, to Countenance this publick Joy.

The Count *de Berka*, and the Heer *Colomma*, the Imperial and Spanish Ministers testified their Satisfaction by Illuminations before their Lodgings: Mijn Heer *Schuylenbergh* did the same at his own House upon the *Viverbergh* with Noble Illuminations, beautified with several Devices: As, *Regi Gulielmo Reduci:* To *King* William *returned again. Transitque feriutque:* He *passes by and strikes. Imperat Augustus:* Augustus Governs. *Superat Cœlestibus alis:* He *mounts with Heavenly Wings. Generosus ab Ortu:* Noble

from

from his Birth. These were to be seen some time after. Others also gave other instances of their Satisfaction, every Man after his own Fancy.

This was also graced with so vast a resort of People, as had never before been seen at the *Hague*: Some coming to see the Solemnity, others to see the King once more returned again, and Crowned with so much Honour.

The King well satisfied with all these their Demonstrations of Esteem and Reverence, immediately applied himself to Business; having first given Audiences of Congratulation to all the Colleges and Deputies of the Cities, and to some great Lords and publick Ministers.

The Elector of *Brandenburgh*, and two Princes of the House of *Anspach*, (who came two days before the publick Entry) were often with the King, and sometimes the Ministers of the other Allies joyned with them: It was said, That three Ruffians were sent from the French Court to cut off the King, and that there were particular Informations given in of their Persons.

February the 7th in the Afternoon the King went into the Assembly of the States General, and took his place as Stadtholder and Captain General; and made an Oration to them, to this purpose.

That

That when His Majesty was last in Council, he acquainted their High and Mightynesses with His Intention to go over into England with the Assistance which they were pleased to give Him, to deliver that Nation from their Impending Dangers, and which in part had befallen them: And that God Almighty had so far Blessed Him, as that He had brought His Affairs to a Happier Issue then at first He could possibly Wish for; for which Reason they offered Him the Crowns of Great Britain and Ireland, which He accepted of, not out of any Ambition, (for He was not to be Corrupted with that, or Money) but only to preserve Religion and Liberty in those Kingdoms; and to be able to give the Allies a vigorous Assistance against the Power of France, which he had given before in a more particular manner, if the Affairs of Ireland had not diverted Him; which being now better settled than they were before, He was now come over, not only to take such Measures with their High and Mighty Lordships, as should be most for the advantage of the Confederates, but also to perform the Duty of Captain General; And that from His tenderest Years He had always a High Regard for that State, and should always be ready to give greater Proofs, if it were possible, how ready He should be to promote their Welfare, for which he would joyfully hazard His Life, if it might be a means to preserve the Liberty of Europe, and to encrease the Felicity of the United Provinces: And finally, He Recommended Himself to the

good

good Wishes of their High and Mighty Lordships.

Hereupon the Lord President Thanked His Majesty in their Lordships Name, for the Honour which was done unto them by his appearing once more in Person amongst them: And he assured him, that they were highly sensible of those Obligations which he had Conferred upon them from time to time, by engaging in so great dangers so readily for their Sakes: And further, that they should always Thankfully Acknowledge how much He had done for them; wishing Him all Happiness in all His Undertakings, promising their Concurrence with His Majesty to the utmost, and that they should contribute whatever they were able, to advance the common Interest, and His Majesties Satisfaction.

He afterwards made a Speech to the States of *Holland*, and was answered much to the same purpose.

The Evening before the King visited the Princess of *Nassaw*, Lady to the Hereditary Stadtholder of *Friezeland*; as also the Princess *Radzevile*, and the Princess of *Saxe-Eysenach*. The next day the King Treated the Elector of *Brandenburgh*, the Duke of *Norfolk*, and several other Lords at the House in the Wood, and returned in the Evening again to the *Hague*.

The

The Ninth in the Morning the Heer *Prielmeyer*, the Envoy of the Elector of *Bavaria*, had Audience of His Majesty; he was Conducted from his Lodgings about Ten a Clock, by the Master of the Ceremonies, with some Coaches and Six Horses, and was received at the Stair-foot by the Swiss Guards placed in Order, and received by their Officer at the end of the Guard Room, and thence conducted through the Anti-Chamber into the Presence; where after he had paid the accoustomed Reverences, he made a Harangue in French to this purpose.

That he was sent by the Elector his Master to Congratulate His Majesties happy Successes; and that his Master had begun his Journey as soon as ever he had heard that His Majesty had begun His; so that he expected him every Hour, to be ready upon the spot to assure His Majesty *of his Readiness to serve the common Cause, and particularly to second those Glorious Undertakings, which His Majesty had so happily begun: And for his part, he only farther begg'd, That his Person might not be unacceptable.*

To this the King replied, *That he Thank'd his Electoral Highness, That he should always endeavour to promote the common Interest: and therefore would joyn with the Elector, and that He was Oblig'd to his Highness for this Trouble; and lastly, that his Person was very acceptable.*

Then the Envoy presented his Gentlemen to the King, who kissed his Hand; and afterwards the Envoy was carried back in the same manner to his Lodgings as he was brought up.

Then the Envoys of *Mentz*, *Cologne*, *Munster* and *Hambourg*, had their publick Audiences, after whom came the Elector of *Brandenburgh*, who had a private Audience of near two Hours.

The Duke Administrator of *Wirtenbergh*, with his Brother, who were there *incognito*, were admitted without Ceremonies.

Also the Deputies of the Cities and Countries, who were obliged to go home to give an account of their Affairs, had their Audience of *Congé* of His Majesty: And afterwards the Pensionary, Secretaries, and Deputies of the States of *Zealand*, had their Audiences, and Complemented the King.

The Count of *Erbagh* came from Prince *Waldeck*, and several Foreign Ministers from the Emperor, the King of *Spain*, the Duke of *Savoy* had their Audiences.

The 12th in the Evening Count *Winditsgratz*, Ambassador Extraordinary from his Imperial Majesty arrived, and had his Audience at Ten a Clock.

The 14th at Noon the King went into the Council of the States, and after some Affairs were dispatched, he went with the Lords Commissioners into the Assembly of their High

High and Mightynesses, where the State of the War for the Year 1691. was presented, which the Deputies were to send down to their respective Provinces; afterwards the King went to Court, and gave Audience to several Foreign Ministers and General Officers, and among the rest to General *Dehvich*.

The 15th the King, with the Duke of *Norfolk*, the Earls of *Portland* and *Devonshire*, with several other Noblemen, Dined with the Elector of *Brandenburgh*: The Elector received the King without, and Conducted him to the Dining-Room. The King went away at Four a Clock, and gave Audience afterwards to the Elector *Palatine*'s Minister. Mr. *Berensdorff* came hither also from the Duke of *Zell*; and Mr. *Klenck* from the Duke of *Hanouer*, to Complement His Majesty in their Masters Names. Prince *Waldeck* came also to Court, and had Audience of the King immediately: And Mr. *Chamgagne* came from the Elector of *Treves*.

The 16th the Elector of *Bavaria* arriv'd, who acquainted the King of his arrival at Ten a Clock, by one of his Gentlemen; he Lodged in his Envoys House: Next Morning my Lord *Portland*, and the Elector of *Brandenburgh* went to Complement him. The Elector was met at the Entrance of the House. About five in the Evening he went privately to the King, and staid about an Hour

Hour and half; and the next day the King returned his Visit.

The 18th in the Evening, the Marquis *de Gaſtanaga*, Governor of the *Spaniſh Netherlands* arrived with a very ſplendid Equipage: As ſoon as he arriv'd he went to Court, and was Received with the Honour due to his Character, the Swiſs Guards being placed in Ranks, with their Officer poſted at the Head of them. He had a particular Audience of the King an Hour long, the Elector of *Bavaria* being by; the Swiſs Guards appeared then in Arms, it being the firſt time that the Elector of *Bavaria* had appeared at Court publickly: The ſame day alſo the Elector of *Brandenburgh* had his Audience: Next Morning the Marquis *de Gaſtanaga* was at the Kings Riſing, and then paid a Viſit to the Elector of *Brandenburgh*; the King was that day above two Hours in the Committee of the Council of State, and Dined with the Elector of *Brandenburgh* at my Lord *Portlands*.

Mr. *Arnauld*, Preacher and Head of the *Vaudois*, who Commanded them ſo bravely againſt the French laſt Summer, came alſo to the *Hague*, and had an Audience of the King concerning their Affairs.

The 19th in the Afternoon the King went a Hawking near *Sorgvliet*, with the Elector of *Brandenburgh*, and ſeveral other Perſons of great Quality: Next Morning he went a Hunting with the Elector of *Bavaria*, and
the

the Marquis of *Gastanaga* near *Hounslaerdyke*, where they Dined, and came back again in the Evening to the *Hague*.

The 20th, the Prince of *Courland*, with another Prince of the House of *Holstein* arrived here.

The 21st, the Landtgrave of *Hesse* came hither with his Envoy, and several other Lords: He immediately went to Court, and staid some time with the King; and the next day he paid a Visit to the Electors of *Brandenburgh* and *Bavaria*. The Duke of *Zalisbach* came also with General *Dautel*, as it's believed, to Complement the King in the Elector *Palatine*'s Name.

The Congress was now often kept: *Colomna* the Spanish Envoy had a Conference on the 23d in the Morning with the Deputies of the States General, and afterwards assisted in the Congress; where was also the Count *Winditsgratz*, the Emperors Plenipotentiary; and the Count *de Berka*, and the Chevalier *Crampricht* the other Imperial Ministers were by, when he show'd his Credentials, and the States assured him, that he should have Audience with the usual Ceremonies in two or three days. The Counsellor *Mean*, who was sent by the Prince and Chapter of *Liege*, assisted also in the Congress, and the Emperors Minister, with most of the other Ministers waited upon his Majesty.

This extraordinary Concourse has made the Court at the *Hague* so very Splendid, that it has out-done any thing else in any other Court of Christendom. Above 30 Sovereign Princes were there, besides Marquesses, Earls, Barons, and Gentlemen without Number. The Elector of *Bavaria*, and the Marquis *de Gastanaga* kept publick Tables.

The 24th, about Ten in the Morning, the Count *de Winditsgratz* had publick Audience of the King, Conducted by the Master of the Ceremonies, with all the usual Solemnities: He Congratulated His Majesties happy Successes, and assured him that the Emperor his Master esteemed himself very much obliged to His Majesty, for that Care and Concern which he show'd for the common Cause; and he further added, that his Master look'd upon His Britannick Majesty, as the principal moving Cause upon whom every thing else depended, that might be for the advantage of the Confederacy.

The Elector of *Saxony*'s Envoy had Audience of the King the same day.

The 25th in the Morning the King, with the Elector of *Brandenburgh*, and the Landtgrave of *Hesse*, went to the great Church, where they heard a Sermon Preached by Mr. *Ulier*; who towards the latter end, said several moving Things to His Majesty. In the Afternoon, the King, with the Electors of *Bavaria* and *Brandenburgh*, and the Landtgrave

grave of *Hesse*, all four in a Coach, took three or four turns round the *Voorhout*, with the Glasses down upon the Kings side, who was received by the thronging Multitudes with all imaginable Demonstrations of Affection and Joy.

The 26th, the Count *de Prela Doria*, Envoy Extraordinary from the Duke of *Savoy*; Count *d'Autel*, with the same Character from the Elector *Palatine*, had Audience of His Majesty, as had on the 27th the Sieur *Haxhuysen* from the Elector of *Saxony*.

March the 5th, the Earl of *Devonshire* Treated the Elector of *Brandenburgh*, the Landtgrave of *Hesse*, the Prince *Commercy*, and divers other Persons of Quality with great Magnificence, where His Majesty was pleased to Honour his Lordship with His Presence.

On the 11th the Duke of *Zell* arrived at the *Hague*, and the Duke of *Wolfembuttel* on the 14th.

During all this time the Congresses had been held almost every day, with great Secrecy, His Majesty always Honouring them with His Presence, when at last, the matters being fully Concerted, and all Things agreed upon to the mutual Satisfaction of all the Princes, this great Council broke up, and the Princes returned to their respective Homes, to put in execution the Designs here agreed upon, the good Effects whereof we doubt not but to see this Campagne, notwithstanding

ing the unhappy accident of the loss of *Mons*.

His Majesty having given Orders to all the Troops to be in a readiness to take the Field by the first of *April*, was pleased on the 16th to depart for *Loo*, being accompanied with the Duke of *Zell*, who Rid in the same Coach with Him, and lay that Night at the House of Monsieur *Zullestein*; where he was met by the Elector of *Bavaria*, who likewise accompanied His Majesty to *Loo*, where they arrived the next Evening, having been Complemented as they passed along with all Demonstrations of Respect and Affection, by the City of *Utrecht*, and the several Towns he pass'd through, and accompanied every where with the loud Acclamations of the People, who were almost overwhelm'd with Joy, at the extraordinary Honour they received by the Presence of this most illustrious Monarch.

But His Majesty had not been long there before he received the unwelcome Tidings of the Siege of *Mons*, an Express arriving at the *Hague* on the 16th in the Evening, that the French Troops had suddenly invested the Town of *Mons*, their Horse having taken Possession of all the Avenues on the 15th of *March*, and that the Foot were marching up with all Diligence.

The Prince of *Steenhuysen*, and the Marquis *Bedmar*, being sent from the Governor of of *Flanders*, arrived at the *Hague* the 17th, and after a short Conference with Prince *Waldeck*, went Post to *Loo*, to give His Majesty an account of the State of the Affair. Who being resolved Himself to Head the Army, in order to raise the Siege, returned to the *Hague*; from whence having dispatched Prince *Waldeck* with necessary Orders for *Flanders*, set forward Himself the 26th for *Brussels*; the Army in the mean time preparing with all imaginable diligence to Muster at *Hall*, whither His Majesty went on the 6th of *April*, intending to have marched the next day at the Head of the Army, which consisted of 30000 Foot and 16000 Horse, with a Train of Artillery of 71 pieces of Cannon and 14 Mortars. But the Carriages not being all come up, was obliged to defer His March for two or three days.

The French had all this time very vigourously attacked the Outworks of the Town, but were as vigourously repulsed by the Besieged, to the great loss of the Enemy, who paid dearly for what he gained; insomuch, that it was not doubted, but the Town would have been able to have held out till the Army came up to its Relief, but the French King (who was himself all the while at St. *Gislain*, near the Camp, the Dauphin Commanding in Chief) according to his old Methods, had found means of gaining a Party among the Burghers and Clergy in the Town,

Town, who prevailing upon the rest, by the terrifying Destruction the Bombs and Cannon made in their Houses, and persuading them that by a timely Surrender of the Town they might obtain Honourable Conditions, made them basely desert the publick Good, and altogether unexpectedly, even to the French themselves, on the 8th of *April*, beat a Parley, and sent out three Officers, as Hostages for three French Officers, who immediately entred the Town, to Treat upon Articles of Surrender; the Governor the Prince *de Bergue* oppos'd the Surrender, and refus'd to deliver the Gate to the French as the Burghers had agreed, endeavouring to disswade them from this their Resolution, alledging he could still hold out till the Relief came; but all would not do, the Burghers were resolved, and they being stronger than the Garison, who were all employed in the Outworks, the Honourable Governor was forced to submit, and about Midnight the Capitulation was Signed on both sides; and the next day *April* the 9th, a Gate of the Town was deliver'd up to the French Guards; and on the 10th, the Garison marched out, being about 4000 Foot and 400 Horse, with Arms, Baggage, Drums beating, Colours flying, six pieces of Cannon, two Mortars, &c. and were conducted to *Tubiese*, a few Miles from *Mons* towards *Brussels*.

The King having received this surprizing News, just as he was ready to march to their Relief,

Relief, was forced to alter his Measures; and understanding that the French King had seperated his Troops, and dispos'd 'em into Garisons; and that he with the Dauphin, &c. were return'd to *Versailles*, broke up the Camp, and having sent Reinforcements to *Charleroy*, *Aeth*, *Namur*, and the other Frontier Garisons, went to *Brussels*; and from thence to the *Hague*, where he was pleased to Honour the Duke of *Zell* (who was likewise return'd thither from the Camp) with the Noble Order of the Garter, who was invested with the Garter and George by the King Himself, assisted by the Dukes of *Norfolk* and *Ormond*, and the Earl of *Devonshire*: This was perform'd privately in the Kings Bed-Chamber the 18th of *April*: And the next day, *Garter* King at Arms presented to his Highness the rest of the Ensigns, with the whole Habit and Ornaments of the Order, which his Highness having Received, was pleased to make a very Noble Present to the King at Arms, and to all the Retinue he had brought with him upon this Occasion.

April the 22d, His Majesty having taken leave of the States General, and been Complimented by them, with all the Expressions of sincere Affection, took Shiping in the *Maese* in order to his Return for *England*, and the Wind being fair, the next Morning made the English Shore; and that Evening, viz. *April* the 13th, 1691. O. S. about
Eight

Eight of the Clock landed at *Whitehall*, having been Saluted by the Fleet, as he passed along with all their Guns, and the repeated Huzza's of the Seamen, who Demonstrated the most extraordinary Joy imaginable; and by the Guns of the Forts of *Tilbury*, *Gravesend*, and the Tower; also by the Ships that lay in the River; and the Joyful Acclamations of the People, who crowded in great Numbers upon the Shore, and in Boats, to see His Majesty, and express their Joy upon his happy Return, continually Repeating,

God Save King William *and Queen* Mary; *and Prosper their Arms by Sea and Land.*

Thus have we finished our short Journal of His Majesties Voyage into *Holland*, wherein we have been as particular as was convenient, and as brief as possible; we have all along carefully avoided all manner of Reflections and Animadversions of our own, and given only a true Relation of the matter of Fact as it occur'd; wherein if we have the good Fortune to please the Reader, we have our End.

FINIS.

www.ingramcontent.com/pod-product-compliance
Lightning Source LLC
Chambersburg PA
CBHW020907230426
43666CB00008B/1350